Till Death

Straight talk for wives: what to do after the "*I do's*"

Inspirational Devotional

Katie King

till DEATH
Straight Talk for Wives: What to do after "I do"
Katie King

Watercress Press

All scripture references used from NIV and NKJV

Table of Contents

46. Sticks and stones

47. Pray without ceasing

48. I trust you

49. Your wish is my command

50. Did you pay the electric bill?

51. I'm exhausted

52. Road blocks

53. This is your sign

54. Drop dead diva

55. Don't ever forget

56. Don't bet on it

57. Pick your battles

58. Drama queen

59. Your cheating heart

60. Dinner time

61. I'm not a mind reader

62. Great expectations

63. It's comfortable

64. A bigger piece of the pie

65. Your serve

66. The bedroom scene

67. Green-eyed monster

68. A gentle answer turns away wrath

69. Grow up

70. Deliver us from temptation

71. Eating crow

72. That's going to leave a mark

73. Man's best friend

74. Time's up

75. I love you to the moon and back

76. Be all that you can be

77. Proverbs 31 woman

A note from the author:

This book is mostly my opinion as the author, but backed up with scripture, and is, therefore, intended to inspire each reader to have the kind of blessed, Godly relationship with his or her spouse as I have with my husband.

Some of the suggestions and discussions in this book may offend some readers, and that is not my intent. Some of the subjects may not even apply to you personally. If a situation does not apply to your marriage, feel free to skip over it with a prayer of thanks that it is not a problem in your marriage, but keep it as reference for later, in case the situation should ever arise.

In today's godless society, it isn't easy having a Godly relationship, but I pray the suggestions and scripture in this book will give you a good foundation in Christ.

My prayer for you is that you will see that the things I have included in this book are the result of the suffering both me and my husband have experienced from making previous bad choices in picking a spouse that wasn't equally yoked with us. Though neither of us believes in divorce, we became victims of it.

Do not be yoked together with unbelievers. For what do righteousness and wickedness have in common? Or what fellowship can light have with darkness?

2 Corinthians 6:14, 15

Now that God has blessed me and my husband with each other, we intend to live our lives as God would have us to be together, and I pray that you will benefit from our lessons learned, and take heart to what does and does not work in relationships from our own experiences.

If you want to improve your marriage, and have a healthy, happy life with your spouse, then this book is for you.

By the time you finish this book, you will either hate me for telling you the truth (because let's face it, the truth can sometimes hurt), or you will thank me for giving you sound, biblical advice that no one else is bold enough to tell you to your face!

In Christ's love, Katie

1

Till death. What next?

The chapters in this book deal with REAL issues that we all face at one time or another, whether in our own marriages, or in the marriages we see in our families and friends. Trust me when I tell you, I do NOT sugar-coat anything for the readers of this book. This is NOT a work of fiction; it's real life and real issues for real people who want to stay married and in love.

Till death means exactly that! No ifs, ands, or buts. Even though both my husband and I are previously divorced, it does NOT mean either of us believes in divorce. It simply means that our ex's didn't believe in the vows they took, and broke them in more ways than one.

Marriage is not easy. It's hard work, and it's not for the faint at heart. Living with another human being and staying in love takes work. I hope that the pages in this book will help you understand what it takes to make that happen. Change begins with YOU.

But at the beginning of creation, God made them male and female. For this reason, a man will leave his father and mother and be united to his wife, and the two become one flesh. So they are no longer two, but one. Therefore, what God has joined together, let man not separate.

Mark 10: 6-9

My prayer for you is that you will read each chapter with total honesty, and if *you* are the problem for that particular subject, it's time to hit your knees and do some sincere praying for God to change your heart. While you're down there, pray for your husband and your marriage, no matter what condition it's in.

God has joined you together, let no man separate you—that applies to the married couple themselves more than anyone else, since it is usually one spouse or the other that causes the separation, but since the two became one, both are responsible for keeping that separation from happening.

Remember, you cannot change your spouse. Only God can. You are only in control of yourself and your own reactions and actions. Make wise choices in your life and in your marriage, because you may not get another chance to fix the things that could break your marriage foundation.

I pray you will read these pages with an open heart, and a willing spirit.

2

We're out of toner

Let's talk about tone of voice. Some people do not know how to change their tone from snotty or condescending to loving and joyful toward their spouses. Start paying attention to the way YOU speak to your spouse. Are you constantly short with him? Do you snap at him when you're tired? Or raise your voice when he asks you to do something for him?

If you do, stop it! Stop it now and pray about it.

Snapping at someone and raising your voice can actually become a habit that needs to be stopped cold-turkey. If you don't, you're going to hurt the man you love. Even if he’s raising his voice or snapping at you, that doesn’t give you the right to do it too.

Each of us is only accountable for his or herself. Think about when you got into trouble as a child, and your parents told you not to tattle. They were only interested in what *you* did wrong. Your sibling, if also guilty, was dealt with separately from you. The same goes for judgment day! When you get before God, and He asks, why were you so short with your husband all the time? Your answer better not be; *well, he was short with me all the time too!*

When judgment day comes along, you want God to say, *‘despite the fact your husband constantly snapped at you and was short with you; you kept quiet and did not fight with him about it’*. Having God tell you He’s proud of you for handling yourself the way His word commands, is far better than any feelings of justification you might get from wrongful actions toward your husband here on earth.

The bible tells us we will be held accountable for every careless word we speak. How many will you be held accountable for?

But I tell you that every man will have to give account on the day of judgment for every careless word they have spoken. For by your words you will be acquitted, and by your words you will be condemned.

Matthew 12:36, 37

3

The honeymoon is over

I hear many of my friends and family using this expression, and I tell them, it doesn't have to be.

There are plenty of ways to keep the newness of your marriage even after your 50th wedding anniversary.

So often, we get so caught up in our lives that we forget to live. Your job is demanding or the kids are too much work, and before you know it, you let little things about your spouse start to irritate you. Before long, you are spending more time being critical of your spouse, and finding fault in him, and less time trying to keep the magic in your relationship.

Think back to your dating days and all the little things that impressed you. Do those things now irritate the heck out of you? If so, then change the way you see your spouse, and ask God to let you see him through divine eyes.

If you let the romance die off in your marriage, it's because YOU aren't doing anything to change it. You might whine that he stopped bringing you flowers, or that he doesn't shave anymore to impress you. Buy the flowers yourself, and put them in the center of the table and have a special dinner when he gets home from work whether he's clean-shaven or not.

If you have kids, try to arrange for them to have dinner *out* with family or a babysitter for the night so you can have a romantic dinner with just the two of you. Put on a nice dress and do your hair and put away the sweat pants for the night. Put on a little music and ask him to dance.

Recreate your first date if necessary. Or sit at home with a good clean movie and a bowl of popcorn, if that's what the two of you do. Whatever it is that you have in common, do that, and keep the conversation rolling. Reminisce about your dating days.

Tell each other all the things you love about each other. Make it a no-fighting-allowed night. Even if all you do is cuddle on the couch, try to get him to do the same under the stars.

Be silly together. Catch lightning bugs, or go fishing. Play cards or take a walk. As long as you make it a point to do something with just the two of you at LEAST once per week, you can keep the honeymoon going.

Date night is an important part of keeping your relationship fresh.

Wives, submit yourselves to your own husband as you do to the Lord. For the husband is the head of the wife as Christ is the head of the church, his body, of which he is the savior. Now as the church submits to Christ, so also wives should submit to their husbands in everything.

Ephesians 5: 22-24

Wives, respect and submit to your husbands so that, if any of them do not believe the word, they may be won over without words by the behavior of their wives, when they see the purity and reverence of your lives.

1 Peter 3: 1, 2

4

I have a headache

I'm going to say it OUT LOUD: don't ever use sex as a weapon! Do not withhold from your partner or use sex as a means to get what you want.

Sex is an expression of love. If it is only sex to you, then you are thinking about it all wrong. It is the blessed union that makes you one with your spouse, and it is to be honored.

If you truly have a headache and your spouse wants to make love to you, take some aspirin, a hot shower, and then let him have it. If you constantly turn him down, it may be a while before he offers again, and the reason could be devastating.

The husband should fulfill his marital duty to his wife, and likewise the wife to her husband. The wife's body does not belong to her alone, but also to her husband. In the same way, the husband's body does not belong to him alone, but also to his wife. Do not deprive each other except by mutual consent and for a time, so that you may devote yourselves to prayer. Then, come together again so that Satan will not tempt you because of your lack of self-control.

1 Corinthians 7: 3-5

If you have to, pray about this. Remember that your body is not your own. It belongs to your husband, and his body belongs to you (in the Godly sense). If the situation is turned around, and your spouse does this to you, and will not see reason to the words in the scripture, pray about it and be loving toward him. Remember not to let anger cause you to sin.

5

Attitude adjustment

When you find yourself getting irritated with your spouse, instead of lashing out, PRAY! Ask God to give you an attitude adjustment. If what you want to say to your spouse does not edify or lift him up, but tear him down instead, you ought not say it at all.

When you were a child, and your mother said to you; *if you don't have anything nice to say, don't say anything at all,* that same principle still works as an adult. In fact, as adults, we should know better by now.

Turn your frown upside-down, and CHOOSE to be happy instead. That's right. I said you have a choice. You can make a bad situation worse, and you can hurt the man you love, or you can choose to be happy and content no matter what your circumstances, and make your spouse happy at the same time.

It's a win-win.

Remember how much you love him, and think to yourself, is fighting about this worth putting a permanent mark against our marriage? Every time you fight with your spouse, you chip away at the foundation of your marriage.

What would you do if he died, or worse, left you of his own free will? Think about that next time you consider opening your mouth about something that won't matter in five minutes' time.

If you think you're unhappy now, think of how unhappy you'll be without him, and ask yourself it that's something you can live with.

No one wants to be around miserable people who have bad attitudes.

Each of us is responsible for our own happiness, and we find that happiness in God first, then our spouses, then our children—in that order.

If you're not happy with your spouse, you're going to have to find something to be happy about, and find it FAST. Every day that ticks by with you having an unhappy feeling, will put a wedge between you. You'll stop talking, and before you know it, you won't kiss or hug or even exist very well together. You will drift apart and it is tough to get that back once it's gone.

Always remember how you felt about him in the beginning, and use that to rebuild your foundation. Laugh at his jokes again even if they have become annoying to you. Look at him through the same rose-colored glasses you looked at him when you first met, and remember how fascinated you were with him, and how infatuated you were, and how much in love you were from the very beginning. These tricks will help you rebuild your foundation with your husband, and might even re-kindle a few new ones.

He is the love of your life, and the one you chose to marry, and that should say something about who he is. If his attitude has changed, it's possible that yours has changed too. Give yourself an attitude adjustment and fall back in love with the man you married.

Finally, brothers, whatever is true, whatever is honorable, whatever is just, whatever is pure, whatever is lovely, whatever is commendable, if there is any excellence, if there is anything worthy of praise, think about these things.

Philippians 4: 8, 9

But I say to you that everyone who is angry with his brother will be liable to judgment; whoever insults his brother will be liable to the Council; and whoever says "You fool!" You will be liable to the hell of fire.

Matthew 5: 22

6

I could be wrong but...

ALWAYS be the first to admit when you're wrong! You heard me correctly. Don't partially admit to faults, or put conditions on your level of wrongness.

After you admit you're wrong, apologize!

Say you were wrong, and say you're sorry if the situation calls for it, which in my experience; the two go hand-in-hand.

Let go of your pride and your stubbornness and be the bigger person. One of you has to apologize, and if it seems like it's always you, that is okay.

Will it hurt you to apologize? No! Could it hurt your marriage if you don't apologize? Absolutely! Why put your marriage at risk over such petty things? Perhaps this time it isn't just a petty thing. Maybe it's a very big thing. But at the end of the day, you have to ask yourself, is being right worth ruining my marriage over this? If it is truly more important to you to be right, then I have no other advice for you except pray about this. If, on the other hand, you are willing to see that being right is not that important, then there is great hope for your marriage.

If you're afraid to admit fault, or admit when you're wrong, or if you refuse to, that can also chip away at your marriage. You don't have to be right all the time.

Long before the days when Google could have saved me embarrassment, my ex would drag out the dictionary or an encyclopedia—just to prove me wrong. All this did was leave me feeling belittled and stupid in his eyes. You should never put your spouse down and then gloat at his inadequacies. In doing this, you're only putting yourself down because you chose him!

Instead, lift him up, and don't upstage him if you do happen to be smarter at something than he is. Don't play dumb either; men know when you're doing this, and it's almost more of an insult.

Don't ever make the admission of guilt to be smug or to rub your spouse's nose in it. After you admit you were wrong and apologize, if necessary, then let the matter drop. Never bring it up, and never use it against your spouse.

Whoever conceals his transgressions will not prosper, but he who confesses and forsakes them will obtain mercy.

Proverbs 28:13

If we confess our sins, he is faithful and just to forgive us our sins and to cleanse us from all unrighteousness.

1 John 1: 9

Let no corrupt talk come out of your mouth, but only such as is good for building up, as fits the occasion, that it may give grace to those who here.

Ephesians 4:29

7

There's no comparison

Never compare your spouse to an old boyfriend or previous spouse if you're divorced. If the new spouse acts the same as the previous person, it may be a flaw in your own choosing of the same type of men. If you keep fighting the same fight, but with a different person, it may be something *you* are doing wrong, or you might be going after the same type.

My sister always went after handsome, hunky bad-boys, and then couldn't understand why they didn't treat her well…enough said!

That doesn't mean you can't find a handsome, hunky man who is a nice guy—I did!

If you do happen to end up with the same type of man, don't say to him; *you're just like my ex.* Let him be his own man, and try treating him and the situation differently than you did with the last one, and maybe you might be able to turn the situation around.

Set the mood for your spouse to be brand new to you, and don't point out inadequacies you believe him to have compared to your ex. Let him be his own person in your eyes. Even if you never say it to him, you should put it out of your mind if you even think it. Ask God to let you see him through His eyes, and to see him with love, rather than contempt.

In the same way, don't compare yourself with others. Don't compare your marriage with the marriage of another couple. You don't know what happens behind closed doors in that marriage, and before you think they have a better marriage than you do, pay better attention to your own marriage. Perhaps they are simply better at concealing their dirty laundry then you are. If you're always so busy thinking that the grass is greener on the other side of the fence, you might miss out on the lush, green lawn and blooming flowers you have in your own backyard.

It is always better not to compare yourself with others.

Love your neighbor as yourself.

Matthew 22:39

We do not dare to clarify or compare ourselves with some who commend themselves. When they measure themselves by themselves, and compare themselves with themselves, they are not wise.

2 Corinthians 10: 12, 13

8

Easy does it

No one ever said marriage was going to be easy. Anything worth having is worth working for, am I right?

Most of us think the little problems we had when we were dating will go away once we marry that person. Often, the opposite is true. Marriage is work. A *good* marriage is a lifetime job and a lifetime commitment. You are not allowed to give up on that person just because you're bored, or you want something else, or you want to put him away like a used toy for the next newest toy on the market. Marriage is not a game. It is one of the biggest commitments that you will have in this lifetime.

If we all had access to that *easy button*, our lives would be very boring. Think about that for a moment. Although you might think that the stresses of your marriage are too much to handle, if you handle them together, they will be less of a burden. Nothing in this life that is worth going after, is so easy to obtain, that it takes no effort at all. You must work every day to keep communication open, and to be sure that you are always kind to your spouse. He may be having a bad day, and it may be worse than your day, but if you're only concerned with yourself, you may miss out on an opportunity to be there for him, and that is your job.

When you're married, your life is not your own. Your life is committed to that person with whom you married.

My husband and I are so in tune with each other, that when one of us is sad the other is sad too. When we are happy, we are both happy. When you have true compassion for your spouse, their ups and downs become your ups and downs. It's all part of the *in good times and bad times* part of your vows. When one of us is sick, the other is completely subservient to the other. But not just in sickness, but also in health. Because in taking care of your spouse when they are healthy, you can help keep them healthier, emotionally and physically.

In doing these things for your spouse, you will build up spiritual fruit for your labor of love.

God is not unjust; he will not forget your work and the love you have shown him because you have helped his people and continue to help them. We want each of you to show the same diligence to the very end; in order to make your hope sure. We do not want you to

become lazy, but to imitate those who through faith and patience inherit what has been promised.

Hebrews 6:9-12

9

Don't let the sun go down

My husband and I have a pact between us; we never go to sleep without telling each other that we love each other, and we always kiss. Even on the occasion when we weren't seeing eye-to-eye on something, we put it away for the night, and kissed and declared our love for one another.

You might say, no way, I'm too mad at him to kiss him, and he probably won't kiss me anyway. I can almost guarantee that if you hugged and kissed your spouse and told him you loved him, you would shock him, if for some reason the two of you were not on speaking terms. Even if he doesn't kiss you back or return the love, you should do it.

Instead of flopping in the bed and turning your backs on one another, kiss and make up—for now. You might discover that after a good night of sleep, that all is forgiven and put away, including the argument you had the night before.

Now, before you say you can't do that, imagine your life without him. Imagine how you would feel if that man died in his sleep, or left you before you got up in the morning and never came back. If the last words you said to him were that you loved him and you kissed him, you could live with your clear conscience.

Don't be stubborn, and don't play the victim. Let go of your pride and tell him you love him, and kiss him. It might be the last chance you get.

In your anger, do not sin. Do not let the sun go down while you are still angry, and do not give the devil a foothold.

Ephesians 4:26, 27

10

Dirty laundry

My husband has this bad habit of leaving his dirty laundry on his side of the bed on the floor! Despite my hints to let him know there is an empty hamper in the bathroom only a few feet from his pile, and despite my many attempts at trying to get him to use the hamper, he prefers to drop the dirty socks and pants on the floor before he gets in bed.

Since anyone who visits our house can see our bedroom from the hall that leads to the living room and kitchen, I prefer that he not leave the pile there.

He leaves it there anyway, and I've learned to let that go and just pick it up if I have to, because in public, he has never embarrassed me by airing dirty laundry.

I was taught growing up not to air your dirty laundry in public, and seeing actual dirty laundry doesn't really count for this discussion…

That being said, have you ever been in public and heard a couple arguing? It's not very pretty to listen to, and sometimes it just makes you want to tell them to go home and settle their differences.

As Christians, we should always make sure that our dirty laundry is not out in the open where others can see. I'm not talking about the physical laundry; I'm talking about your personal business. If you have a disagreement in public and start screaming at each other, what does that say about you? That goes the same with the children. Discipline them when you get home. I have seen civil wars break out in restaurants where one parent will start yelling at the children, and before you know it, the entire family is screaming at each other.

Another word of advice: don't yell at your husband or belittle him in front of his friends, or either of your families, or complain about him in front of them. There are certain moral boundaries you should never cross, and that's one of them. Even if he does something to make you angry; let it go until you are in private, and until you get to a private place where the two of you can talk, do NOT treat him badly in front of this friends or either family. You can get mad at him when you get home, but hopefully, by the time you get there, you'll have forgotten all about it and it won't matter anymore. Forgive him and let it go.

I was once in a grocery store where two sisters (adults) began to argue, and they started slinging poo-words at each other over some man they both liked, and before I realized, they had each picked up cans of green beans and were hitting each other in the head with them. I was shocked and took my kids out of the store, fearing for our safety. It was a good lesson to teach my son and daughter, but it was something I wish I could erase from my memory.

Some things you just can't un-see!

No one wants to see someone else's dirty laundry. Think about that next time you get upset with your spouse when you're out in public.

Ask yourself if fighting over it is worth losing your marriage over, because if it isn't, it's best to let it go and pray about it.

A fool finds no pleasure in understanding, but delights in airing his own opinions.

Proverbs 18:2

11

Pouring salt in the wound

Bringing up past arguments or wrong-doings to your spouse to use as weapons in a current argument is unfair, to say the least. If he were to do the same thing, how would you like it? If he does, talk to him about it and tell him you *both* need to stop doing that because it's hurting your marriage. Agree to try your best, and all you can expect is the same from him.

Whatever is in the past, especially if you have forgiven your spouse for it, is best kept in the past. If, however, your spouse continues to make the same awful mistake, perhaps the two of you need to pray about it in order to keep it from happening again. If you have to forgive him seventy times seven, the way it says to in the Bible, then that is what you will have to do. If not, your marriage will greatly suffer.

If you continue to bring up the matter, even though the current argument may have nothing to do with the previous problem, all you're doing is pouring salt in his wounds—and your own. True forgiveness involves never bringing up the matter again. If the matter continues to come up because it is a constant problem, let each incident be forgiven on its own and dropped accordingly.

Think about your life for just a moment. If your parents brought up every little thing you did wrong from the time you were old enough to walk and talk to your present day, would it get tiring hearing that constantly over and over? You would get tired of hearing about it every time you talked to them, wouldn't you? The same goes for the way you treat your spouse. Let each day be a new day, and a new opportunity to love your spouse and help him to change if he has a bad habit.

My husband had a bad habit of leaving on a trail of lights throughout the house wherever he would go. The man wouldn't turn off the light after he left the room if his life depended on it. As our electric bill grew larger, my patience grew weary. I began to say something to him every time he left a light on. He tried to explain to me that all that reminding him was more irritating than him leaving the light on. I never said it in an unkind way, but the constant reminders began to upset him.

He asked me to simply turn off the lights behind him when he forgot, without saying another word about it. I did as he asked me to, and believe it or not, he turns off lights every time he leaves the room now. I even joke with him that he reaches for the light switch in the daytime. It has become a habit for him now to turn off the light, but no amount of me nagging him would have ever gotten him to stop. It was my silent and subtle act of turning off that light behind him every time that made him sit up and take notice.

In the same way, you must be silent and subtle about things that your husband does that you don't like. Nagging him will only pour salt in the wound, and it will make the wound greater for both of you. Nagging won't change a thing, as I found out with the light switch situation in my own home. All it did was put unnecessary hurt feelings between us that didn't need to be there over such a petty offense. It actually takes less effort to turn off that light switch yourself than to nag him. All that does is cause strife between you, and it doesn't need to be there.

A wife of noble character is her husband's crown, but a disgraceful wife is like decay in his bones.

Proverbs 12:4

Better to live on a corner of the roof, than to share a house with a quarrelsome wife.

Proverbs 25:24

12

Whisper sweet nothings

It's always a good thing to tell your spouse how much you love him. But let's take that a step further, and let's think about all the things you still love about him. It's not enough to say that you love that person if you don't have reasons with which to back it.

For example; I love that my husband is generous, and I tell him that constantly. When you tell your husband thank you for taking out the trash (something that he does all the time), it begins to build an appreciation for him. Get into the habit of telling him thank you for everything he does. I don't mean for you to pat him on the head like a dog. I mean for you to really appreciate the fact that YOU didn't have to take out that trash, and how grateful you are that HE will.

Tell him what a good man he is and compliment him on being a great dad, or whatever it is that you like best about him. You should complement him at least once per day. Do it so often that there is no room for complaining about him.

I tell my husband thank you for picking up after himself (something he should do anyway, right?), but if all you do is complain about what he does NOT do, he will rebel and really do nothing. Then you'll be stuck taking out that trash yourself. When you ask him to do something, ask him nicely, and use the word, *please*. Ask him as if you're asking someone who isn't so close to you.

At the end of my previous marriage, I realized that my ex was kinder to strangers on the street than he was to me. He was very critical, and never complimented, but always put me down. But I came to realize, in his eyes, I would never be pretty enough, strong enough, young enough, smart enough {fill in the blank}, to satisfy him because he was a miserable human being. You know what they say, misery loves company. That was one bit of company I was happy to have out of my life.

When we don't appreciate our spouses, or their efforts to contribute to the welfare of the household, we hurt ourselves just as much, if not more, than we hurt them.

Now, we ask you to respect those who work hard among you, who are over you in the Lord, and who admonish you. Hold them in the highest regard in love because of their work.

1 Thessalonians 5: 12, 13

13

Don’t be a doormat

Being submissive to your husband does not mean being a doormat that he can use to his own benefit. My ex seemed to think it meant exactly that. I’ve had my Bible thrown at me by him, and told that I wasn’t being exactly like it said in *my* Bible. I tried to show him the love of Christ, but he used it against me for his benefit.

My current husband is nothing like that. He believes in being submissive to me too. And I like that. We will each get each other coffee, or serve the other in any way, and he’s such a gentleman, he holds open the door for me, and always walks me down stairs, etc. He takes care of me, and I take care of him, because that is the way marriage is supposed to be. It is not one spouse, usually thought to be the woman, waiting on the other. There isn't one thing that we won't do together. Whether it be washing dishes or working on the lawn.

Find some common ground with your husband, and learn to grow with that.

Wives, submit to your husbands, as is fitting to the Lord.

Colossians 3: 18

Wives, submit to your husbands as to the Lord. For the husband is the head of the wife as Christ is the head of the church, his body, of which he is the Savior. Now as the church submits to Christ, so also wives should submit to their husbands in everything.

Ephesians 5: 22-24

If you think for minute you don't have to, or shouldn't have to, submit to your husband, you're wrong. Being submissive is not old-fashioned. It might not be very popular in today's empowered-woman society, but it *is* biblical.

Don't mistake submissiveness with being a doormat. And it doesn't mean you have to do everything he says; but if he's a fair and Godly man, he would never ask you to do anything that was to put you in a place that made you feel more like his servant than his wife.

In my marriage, we are both servants to each other, and that is what works for us. There isn't one thing that either of us wouldn't do for the other, and that is what being submissive is all about. It's a willingness to submit to the authority in Christ that your husband has over you.

If he *Lords* it over you, that is between him and God. In the end, you are only accountable for yourself.

14

Stop complaining

I truly believe that the more you find to complain about, the more you find to complain about.

Let me explain!

I hear so many women complaining about their husbands, but they don't realize that they were the same women who used to speak so adoringly about their husbands. Once you start complaining about anything—it doesn't even have to be about your spouse—you seem to find fault in everything.

When you find yourself complaining about something, stop and turn it into a positive. No matter how hard this is, make it a challenge if you must, but do it. Force yourself if you have to. If you are constantly complaining about your spouse, or even to your spouse about himself, that is going to get tiring. Something is going to break.

Complaining is another one of those subtle chippers that chips away at the foundation of your marriage. Complainers are miserable to be around. Surely you know someone who is a constant complainer. If that person is you, it's not too late to turn it around.

Pray about it. Ask God to show you every time you start to complain so you can stop yourself and turn that complaint into a compliment.

Do not spend so much time pointing out your mate's faults that you forget to point out his good points. Complaining only brings us more things to complain about, and before you know it, you're spending your whole life complaining. Your whole life becomes one big complaint.

Do everything without complaining or grumbling, so that you may become blameless and pure, children of God without fault in a crooked and depraved generation, in which you shine like stars in the universe.

Philippians 2: 14, 15

15

Pride cometh before a fall

A lot of times, we let pride get in the way of doing what God's will is in our marriages. Often times, we get so caught up in the ways of the world that we forget the basic, yet so meaningful teachings about marriage the Bible offers us. We are often so determined to do things our way, and go with the crowd and whatever is popular, that we get prideful and take credit where God has gotten us through our circumstances.

The Bible tells us that God will never leave us nor forsake us, but yet for something so important as our marriage, we often times think we can handle it ourselves and we push God out. If we don't have a good foundation for our marriage, it will fall apart.

"Anyone who listens to my teaching and follows it is wise, like a person who builds a house on solid rock. Though the rain comes in torrents and the floodwaters rise and the winds beat against that house, it won't collapse because its foundation is built on solid rock. But anyone who hears my teaching and doesn't obey it is foolish, like a person who builds a house on sand. When the rains and floods come and the winds beat against that house, it will collapse with a mighty crash."

Matthew 7: 24-27

Building your marriage on the solid rock of God's word will have the same results in your marriage.

16

Do not love the world

Too often, we put more importance on the things of this world, rather than with the people in our lives that we love. We want bigger faster computers, a faster car, and bigger, more luxurious homes. We get ourselves so deep in debt, that we don't realize the deepest debt we've put ourselves into is a deficit in our marriage. When all we do is gather the things of this world, we forget to gather the things that money can't buy.

I would much rather have one smile from my husband, and a hug and kiss from him, than to have the biggest house in the world without him. What good are all those things if you don't have someone to share them with? And if all you do is spend money just as fast as it comes in to the house, then all you're doing is working to live and living to work!

You will spend your entire lives at work, rather than be able to take vacations, or even retire. You'll be so busy paying for all of those things that you've gathered along the way, that you miss out on the most important thing in life, and that's having loved ones around you. If you have no time to spend with your husband, because you're both working overtime to pay for all the stuff that sits in your house alone while you're at work, ask yourself how much sense that makes.

Instead, you should live within your means, or even possibly below your means, so that you have money to spare, and spend on doing activities to have quality time together. How much fun can it possibly be if all you do is work, while all of your things sit at home alone without you? There is no point in having those things, especially when neither of you gets the opportunity to enjoy them.

How many hours of awake time are you at work versus how many you are at home? When you get home after a long day at work, are you so tired you collapse on the sofa, or fall asleep eating your dinner? That is no way to live, especially not for the sake of having more things around us that are meaningless.

Take an inventory of your closet right now. How many pieces of clothing do you own with the tags still on them? Those items represent an investment in your future that you're losing out on because it's sitting in your closet now worth next to nothing. The tag on it may say that it cost $100, but to sell it secondhand in a garage sale, or at a consignment shop, you would get pennies on the dollar for it. That item represents money you might as well have flushed down the toilet, because that is all it's worth.

From now on, think of the things that money can't buy, such as the love and adoration of your spouse. When he sees that you put more stock in him and your marriage than you do in the things of this world, you will have one happy and secure husband on your hands.

It's a proven fact that the husbands worry more about money than the wives do. And yet it seems that the wives are the ones that are always spending every bit of extra money. So that should tell you that your husband is wise in determining the finances. If he has said to you on more than one occasion to stop buying things and stop wasting money, or if he's ever asked you, '*do you really need this?*', then it's possible that he truly feels this way, and has not said anything other than dropping subtle hints, hoping you might get it. Let your husband's subtle hints be the clue to make you turn your finances around and stop putting your stock in the things of this world and start putting them in *him*.

Do not love the world or anything in the world; if anyone loves the world, the love of the father is not in him. For everything in the world—the cravings of sinful man, the lust of his eyes and the boasting of what he has and does—comes not from the Father but from the world. The world and its desires pass away, but the man who does the will of God lives forever.

1 John 2: 15-17

17

Coffee talk

Communication is the key here. If a marriage lacks communication, it might as will be dead. Keeping the lines of communication open is not as easy as it seems. When a couple gets set in their ways, they tend to simply exist together, and often times, conversation isn't always needed in order to meet each other's needs. You get to a point where you simply know what the other person is going to do and what they need. That sort of intuition with your mate should not replace proper communication.

Instead, set aside time with your husband and bring him a cup of coffee. Sit with him and sip coffee while you talk, even if it's only for five minutes a day. As long as that time is uninterrupted by electronics, the neighbors, family, or even your own children. Just be sure that you have at least a few minutes together every day to talk and catch up with one another.

You can talk about the birds in the backyard, or an upcoming vacation you plan to take. Do not discuss world events or other stressful topics during that time. Let that time together be your safe-zone, to communicate and connect with one another on a personal level. If the two of you can't find five minutes together alone every day, then you're doing something wrong. It should not be so difficult to find that amount of time to spend together.

My husband and I spend our coffee time either in bed, or on the front porch, every morning, but we take that time. When our lives become busy and we get bogged down by appointments and such, we really miss that time together.

You may not be able to take that time every day, but please, for the sake of your marriage, take it as often as possible. Make sure you are both willing to turn off the TV, leave your phones off, and even lock your bedroom door, if that's what it takes. Just to be sure that time is free from any interruptions. Even if all you do is sit and enjoy each other's company in the beginning, make sure you cuddle and connect somehow.

My husband and I, don't like having to give up that cuddle time with each other because of appointments or other obligations, but sometimes it's necessary. When those times occur, try to make up the time later that day or spend a few extra minutes the following day.

Just be certain that it's a promise that you keep to your spouse. If your spouse opened up to you emotionally during this time, don't ever discount or belittle his feelings. It is harder for men to open up emotionally than it is for women, and if you can get your husband to open up to you, then you've won more than half the battle.

The wisest of women builds her house, but with her own hands the foolish one tears hers down.

Proverbs 14:1

18

The way to a man’s heart

My husband has a theory, and it's not well known to women, but apparently it’s very well known to men. He claims that spaghetti fixes everything. Recently, we had an opportunity to put this to the test. He went through a bit of trouble from a family member, and he was very down in the mouth. I remembered what he'd told me years ago, and made a big pot of spaghetti for him. When I presented it to him, I reminded him of what he'd told me, and it put a smile on his face that I had remembered what he'd shared with me. I was so delighted to see that such a simple gesture had made his heart lighter, that I decided that I would put this into practice more often. If spaghetti truly fixes everything, then I will do my best to make sure I have the fixings for it on hand at all times.

There are other ways, other than food, to get to your man's heart. Loving him unconditionally is a big start. Believe it or not, loving someone unconditionally is not as easy as it sounds. In theory, we say that we can do such a thing, but yet we constantly find fault in a mate, and often times they fall short of that unconditional love. Loving someone unconditionally truly means that you love him heart, mind, body, soul, and spirit.

Let's start with his heart. Most men are true romantics at heart, and because of this, they have very big hearts. I think they *naturally* have big hearts. There are some who are heartless, but I'm going to assume for the sake of this discussion, that your husband has a very big heart for you. It seems logical, that if you are the type of woman who is reading this book, that means that you have a very big heart as well. Usually, people who have big hearts, tend to find one another.

Unfortunately, for me and my husband, we didn't find each other until after we both suffered huge heartache. I suppose that's why we both take such care with each other's hearts. We both know how it feels to be hurt by someone, and so we make every effort to try not to do that to each other.

Jesus declared, "love the Lord your God with all your heart and with all your soul and with all your mind."

Matthew 22:37

Because we are a product of our creator, and God is in us, we should love each other in the same way.

19

Accusations fly

Do not ever accuse, without just cause. When we accuse our mate of things that we are not 100% sure of, it will put a wedge between us.

There are instances when wives do know 100% sure, such as in my case, when I discovered my husband sleeping with someone else in my own home. Those things are not only undeniable, but in my opinion, are unpardonable in a marital setting if the sinner will not turn from his wicked, adulterous ways. That is not to say they are not forgivable sins, but only through the grace of God are you able to forgive such a transgression.

All too often, it is jealousy that causes our mate to make accusations. Other times, it is out of anger and frustration. Take heed, and do not repay evil with evil. Most of all, make sure you are not the one doing the accusing. Even if the person is guilty, what is the point of making accusations if not to cause a fight? You should never fight with your spouse. That is not to say that you cannot disagree, but you should never fight. If you or your spouse starts a fight or constantly picks fights, learn to walk away, and don't indulge in giving the devil a foothold in your marriage.

Do not falsely accuse during an argument with your spouse, or if you falsely accuse your husband, without evidence, it could be the ruin of your marriage. Please be careful what you say to one another. Speak in love and speak words that edify and bring life. Never tear down your husband with accusations. Only God is the One True judge, and it is not your place to accuse.

But in that coming day no weapon turned against you will succeed. You will silence every voice raised up to accuse you. These benefits are enjoyed by the servants of the Lord; their vindication will come from me. I, the Lord, have spoken!

Isaiah 54:17

Have a good conscience, so that, when you are slandered, those who defile your good behavior in Christ may be put to shame.

1 Peter 3:16

20

Baby talk

Adding children to the marriage is not always easy, especially if your spouse does not believe in raising those children the same way you do. As present or future parents, you owe it to your children to be a united front where those children are concerned.

When one parent plays *good cop/bad cop* with the children, one parent always suffers, but so do the children. You must NEVER undermine each other in front of your children, nor should you throw the other parent under the bus, so to speak.

Be a united front regarding moral lessons, spirituality, and discipline. My own father used to *pass the buck* to my mother, and they never backed each other up. They would ping-pong me and my siblings between them, and often times the result was double punishments—a direct result of no communication between them. Mom was too lenient and Dad was too harsh, and then they would fight over it—in front of us.

Parents should NEVER argue in front of their children on ANY subject. Think back to your own childhood. If your parents fought in front of you, then remember how badly that made you feel when you do that in front of your own children.

Another thing you should never ever do is to use your kids as a weapon against your spouse. Don't belittle the other parent in front of them. That child is a reflection of BOTH of you, and that child will feel bad by association if their other parent is considered *bad* in your eyes. Don't put the child down and tell him or her they are just like their father if they do something bad. Tell them the good things they do that are like that parent.

Most of all, don't EVER teach your child to hate, disrespect, or defy the other parent in any way. It might just come back to bite you in the booty later!

Train a child in the way he should go, and when he is old he will not depart from it.

Proverbs 22:6

Fathers, do not exasperate your children; instead bring them up in the training and instruction of the Lord.

Ephesians 64

Fathers, do not provoke your children so that they will lose heart and become discouraged.

Colossians 3:21

Those scriptures may be aimed at the father, but I believe they apply to mothers as well.

21

That still, quiet voice

I'm talking about your ability to hear God's voice here. If all you're doing is hollering in your marriage, you'll miss out on hearing God's still, small voice whispering in your ear the instructions for handling just such an emergency.

Then he said, "Go out, and stand on the mountain before the Lord." And behold, the Lord passed by, and a great and strong wind tore into the mountains and broke the rocks into pieces before the Lord, but the Lord was not in the wind; and after the wind was an earthquake, but the Lord was not in the earthquake; and after the earthquake, a fire, but the Lord was not in the fire; and after the fire, a still small voice.

1 Kings 19:11-12

Strife in a marriage is like having a thorn in your side. All that anger and arguing blocks out God's voice in your marriage and can lead to grudges. Holding a grudge can do harm to your relationship with God.

Avoiding strife brings a man honor, but every fool is quarrelsome.

Proverbs 20:3

This goes back to what I said earlier about not fighting with your spouse. Fighting only breeds strife, and strife breeds grudges. You might be sitting here wondering, how in the world can I avoid an argument when that's all my spouse does is fight with me? The answer is simple. It's as simple as keeping your mouth shut. You don't sling insults, and you don't raise your voice. You don't give in to the earthquake or the wind or the fire; you wait for that still, small voice of God to bail you out, and the only way you can hear him, is if you are quiet!

The lips of fools bring them strife, and their mouths invite a beating. The mouths of fools are their undoing, and their lips are a snare to their very lives.

Proverbs 18:6–7

Avoiding fights with your spouse takes a lot of self-control. But it also takes a lot of prayer. Forgive all wrongs and wipe hatred, anger, and un-forgiveness from your heart where your spouse is concerned, and you will succeed.

22

You're wrong

This is another point I can't stress enough. Do NOT point out your spouse's faults. If by some miracle, you've transformed to a *perfect* human, then you might have room to talk. But since none of us is prefect, we have enough of our own faults to point out and work on.

Do not judge, or you will be judged. For with the same judgment you pronounce, you will be judged; and with the measure you use, it will be measured to you.

Why do you look at the speck in your brother's eye, but fail to notice the beam in your own eye? How can you say to your brother, 'Let me take the speck out of your eye,' while there is still a beam in your own eye?

You hypocrite! First take the beam out of your own eye, and then you will see clearly to remove the speck from your brother's eye.

Matthew 7: 1-5

We often times are so concerned with what our spouses are doing wrong in the marriage, that we fail to see the part that WE play in the breakdown and destruction of our marriages.

I can't stress this enough; each of us can only be held accountable for ourselves (which is more than enough!), and likewise, can only work on our own faults.

You can NOT change another human being, only God can. You can pray for that person, and you can change yourself, which in turn, might change things for the better.

Often times, if you change the way you SEE things, and the way you think about them, you help pave the way for a healthy marriage.

23

Humble pie

Don't be afraid to humble yourself in your marriage. I realize this leaves you vulnerable, but if you don't, you will not develop the deep emotional connection that will make your marriage solid as a rock.

Eating a slice of humble pie is certainly easier going down than having to eat crow later!

Whoever exalts himself will be humbled, and whoever humbles himself will be exalted.

Matthew 23: 12

I don't know about you, but I take that as a strict warning! There are times when in the marriage situation, we try to make ourselves look better than our spouses, especially if there is trouble. Don't be part of the problem. Be part of the solution. Be willing to humble yourself in order to keep from being knocked down a few pegs. Stay on your feet; it's a lot easier than having to pick yourself up and dust yourself off (and a lot less embarrassing).

Don't try to be superior over your spouse, whether it be that you make more money than he does, or that you're better at changing a diaper than he is. There are things he might be better at than you are, such as making that baby laugh—and you too, if you give him half a chance.

If you are too competitive, and always have to *one-up* your spouse, or be the best at everything, you won't be much fun to be around.

Always present your spouse in a better light than yourself—especially to others.

Instead of tearing down, lift your mate above yourself, and in doing so, you will be exalted.

24

Be joyful always

We are responsible for our own happiness. The Bible tells us to be joyful always, and this is not always a feat easy to achieve, but I assure you, it's achievable.

No one wants to be around someone who is always unhappy with everything. The Bible teaches us to be content in our circumstances, and in doing so, joy will come in the morning.

If you are depending on your spouse, or a new car, or that position at work you've been pining for to make you happy, you will be miserable if none of that works out for you. If your car is on its last mile, and your promotion was handed to someone else, and your spouse is often-times in his own little world (perhaps stressed about the same things you're stressing over), then you've got to find some happiness in all that, or you are going to fall apart at the seams.

Take delight in the things you can control, and let go of the things you can't. Your own happiness is within your control. Put on a funny movie and laugh together. Take a walk outside (yes, where there are birds that chirp and a sun that will brighten your day), and just hold hands and enjoy each other. Enjoy your life, one minute at a time, if that's what it takes.

If there is ever a time when you look at your life and think you don't have much to be joyful over, think again. You might be one mortgage payment away from foreclosure, your child may have gotten expelled from school, you may have a loved-one who is not doing well health-wise, or you may have just lost your job, and your car died and you left it on the side of the road, or the whole weight of the world may seem like it's crushing you…no matter what your problems, or the circumstances, you have air in your lungs, and the sun came up today, but most of all, God did not fall off his throne!

God is still there waiting for you, and will welcome you with open arms of love, and He will bring joy to your heart if you ask Him. All you have to do is ask.

Always be joyful. Never stop praying. Be thankful in *all* circumstances, for this is God's will for you who belong to Christ Jesus.

1 Thessalonians 5: 16-18

25

Sorry seems to be the hardest word

Why is it that one of the most important things we can say in our marriage is the hardest to belt out?

Saying you're sorry does not make you at fault.

Sometimes, it's okay to say *I'm sorry* in order to avoid an argument. If you brought up a subject that has hit a nerve and your husband gets upset, then perhaps you should apologize. If he's angry because you ran up the credit card bill and he can't pay it, you should probably apologize and make him spaghetti for a week to make up for it (see chapter 18).

Always be the first to say you're sorry. Not to rub it in his face, but to set an example. Some men seem to have trouble saying that word—and some women too.

If you say sorry even when it isn't your fault, it might make the mood a little easier to bear. Don't be a repeat apologizer, and don't be a martyr about it. Be sincere when you apologize.

The worst thing you can do is to give a back-handed apology, and that goes something like this: *I'm sorry IF I hurt your feelings,* or, *I'm sorry IF (fill in the blank).* No matter if you think he's wrong, he feels he's right, and they are his feelings. You should never tell your spouse he doesn't have a right to his own feelings and emotions.

Never tell your spouse to *get over it,* and never tell him you're *not* sorry. This implies *intent to do harm* to him, and it may end your marriage.

Therefore, confess your sins to one another, and pray for one another so that you may be healed. The effective prayer of a righteous man can accomplish much.

James 5: 16

If we confess our sins, He is faithful and righteous to forgive us our sins and to cleanse us from all unrighteousness.

1 John 1: 9

26

The unpardonable sins

Let's get this over with…

God, Himself, has a list of 7 things he calls abominations. Things He hates! On that list are…you guessed it…violence, lying, pride, discord, all forms of wickedness, and evil practices; things that will destroy a marriage.

Also, there is reference to divorce and violence in a marriage, which He also claims to hate.

"I hate divorce," says the Lord God of Israel, "and I hate a man's covering himself with violence as well as with his garment," says the Lord Almighty. So guard yourself in your spirit, and do not break faith.

Malachi 2: 16

Though, in *my* opinion, these are unpardonable sins, they are not unforgivable.

Pardon the expression, but if you are married to what most refer to as a *beater-cheater* like I was, then you'll understand that staying in that marriage is not always an easy decision, and it is always ultimately up to you.

I tried to stay in mine, and I forgave him beyond the seventy-seven times seven rule, but in the end, it was my ex who made that decision for me. He wanted out so he could pursue someone else. Whew! Dodged that bullet (nearly literally, but that is for another book—maybe!)

The ONLY advice I can give you here is to pray until God gives you the answer. I fasted and prayed for thirty days until I got my answer. I think another day, and I wouldn't be here to talk about it today. I drank very little milk in the beginning, but by the end of the journey, I was strictly drinking clear juices and about a gallon of water a day.

Honestly, I have no idea how I made it through the thirty days, except by the grace of God. He got me through it because it was something I had to do. I really never had so much energy and clarity of mind than in that time of fasting and prayer. Each person is different, so I would recommend checking with your doctor before embarking on such a long spiritual fast as this.

In the end, the decision was made for me, and it was the best thing that happened in my life. It freed me from something I didn't want any part of, and it opened the door for the wonderful husband I have now.

27

A word about "Fake-book"

Social media has become a place where everyone can be something they are not. After all, if it's online, then it must be true, right?

Wrong!

My husband and I know too many (family members!) who make themselves look like victims on social media, and everyone is fast to jump on there and say, oh you poor thing.

On social media, you can be the best wife, mom, athlete, friend, sister, employee, etc., when in reality, none of it is true.

Do NOT use social media to belittle your mate, or to make yourself look better than you are. Be yourself up there, and if being yourself isn't good enough to be in the public eye the way you are, then you better do something to change that.

If you post pictures to save-face with family to make it look like you have the perfect marriage and the perfect family, STOP what you are doing, because you're creating this dangerous world for yourself that is not real.

I treat social media the same way I treat my bathroom habits. I get in, take care of my business, and get out.

LOL!

Get the *fake* off of social media, and BE that great mom, and BE that perfect wife, daughter, friend, employee, etc.

For there is nothing hidden that will not be disclosed, and nothing concealed that will not be known or brought out into the open.

Luke 8: 17

For God will bring every deed into judgment, with every secret thing, whether good or evil.

Ecclesiastes 12: 14

Truthful lips endure forever, but a lying tongue, only a moment.

Proverbs 12: 19

28

Sleight of hand

Games have no place in your marriage. Do not say one thing and then do another. Keep your word, and don't create problems where there are none.

When I first became friends with my current husband, before we began dating, he would tell me stories about his ex, and how she would twist things around to get him to believe that he had done whatever wrong she'd done. He said it almost reminded him of a magic trick. The way that she could twist and turn another person's words and make them believe they were the wrongdoers instead of her. Unfortunate for me, I became painfully aware of that trait in her after our first meeting. He'd watched her do this to a lot of people during his entire relationship with her, and when she began to turn her trickster ways against him, he realized she was not the one for him.

With me, I was so trusting of my ex, that he would commit his sins right under my very nose. I'm sure there were subtle hints, but I trusted him and wasn't looking for them, and therefore didn't find them until it was too late. The damage was done, but my eyes were finally open to the tricks he'd been playing on me at my expense.

Often times when a marriage is strong, Satan plays tricks on our minds to make us believe that our spouses are doing wrong behind our backs. You must resist these voices, and pray them away. If you find yourself becoming suspicious when your spouse has given you no reason to be suspicious, then you need to pray about it.

On the other side of that, if you think there is some truth to your suspicions, then by all means you need to pray about that as well until God gives you an answer. Do not bring trouble where there may not be any by investigating something that might not be. Too many times our minds play tricks on us making us believe that we can't trust our mate.

Let's think about that logically for a moment. Unless you have knowledge that your husband is actively engaging in some wrongdoing, I don't think that you should be worrying unnecessarily. The Bible tells us not to borrow trouble and not to let the devil get a foothold in our lives. In everything you do, pray, and pray without ceasing.

When you trust your husband, it keeps peace in your marriage. Do not allow the devil and his tricks to cause you to have a broken marriage. Jealousy can play and ugly part in that, and it's something you need to learn to control before it's too late.

There is no fear in love, but perfect love casts out fear. Fear has to do with punishment, and whoever fears has not been perfected in love.

1 John 4:18

29

Kiss and tell

I cannot stress this enough; kiss your spouse as often as possible, and tell him how much you love and adore him, and how much he means to you. Build each other up in love so that you may stay strong in your marriage.

My husband and I rarely, if ever, see other couples kissing and holding hands, and being as cuddly out in public as we are. I know that there's an unspoken rule about public displays of affection, but as long as you're tactful, a few innocent, quick kisses and holding hands is not only harmless to the eyes, but it is nourishing to the souls of others who watch in adoration of your love that you have for one another.

Men stand up and take notice when they see my husband pulling a chair out for me at a restaurant, or opening my car door for me when I get in. Our neighbors all around us watch in awe as my husband holds my hand while we take walks around the neighborhood.

I know some of these things seem a bit old-fashioned, but there is nothing wrong with showing each other how much you love each other.

Greet one another with the kiss of love. Peace to all of you who are in Christ.

1 Peter 5:14

30

Time out!

My husband and I had to incorporate the “time out” rule in our home, but not for the reason you might think. When my ex began to cause trouble for me and my husband by way of our children, the events became so overwhelming that we were consumed with conversation about it for months on end. It got to be so bad, that we decided when we had enough of talking about it ourselves, or hearing about it from well-meaning family members; we initiated the time-out clause, allowing us time where there was no talk, and no thought of the stress that was going on in our lives. Sometimes, it is the outside stresses that cause us to need a time-out the most.

I recommend to all of you, whenever you are feeling overwhelmed by any situation, or any discussion with your spouse, that you incorporate this strategy long before it becomes an issue, that the two of you are entitled to call time-out! What this does, is allow you to free your thoughts and your emotions, and put the problems away for a time, and then pick them back up later once you've had a chance to breathe.

Sometimes, we need to take a break from the constant stress, and realize there are other more important things in life to deal with. This is where the time-out clause comes in handy. As long as neither party abuses this privilege, it is a handy tool for squelching fights before they begin.

Be not quick in your spirit to become angry, for anger lodges in the hearts of fools.

Ecclesiastes 7:9

Taking a time-out, rather than being quick to anger, can often be a saving factor in your relationship.

31

A woman of virtue

Wikipedia describes **modesty** as *demureness as a mode of dress and deportment intended to avoid encouraging sexual attraction in others; actual standards vary widely. In this use, it can be considered inappropriate or immodest to reveal certain parts of the body.*

The Bible tells us, as women, we are to dress modestly to show our virtue rather than our bodies. Yet I look around this world, and I see nothing but women flashing their flesh for all to see. Mothers are letting their *little girls* wear shorts short enough to be considered underwear, with slogans such as "Juicy" written across the bottom! If that doesn't turn the heads of every pervert out there, I don't know what will.

Don't raise your daughters to accept inappropriate clothing as the norm; you are responsible for their safety, and if you're dressing in a manner to gain attention, think of the attention your little girl is getting. Pay attention to men's stares (grown men), and see if you don't think it's important to protect your daughter. That begins with you, as her mother.

As women and moms, we need to make sure that we are conservative in our dress. The flesh is really for our husband's eyes only. You may make excuses that it's hotter than the sun today, but there are ways to be conservative without showing off so much flesh.

My husband and I watch old shows and movies, and laugh at the costumes they wore as bathing wear on the beach, but really, that is how it should be now. Nowadays it's considered acceptable for a woman to have her whole booty uncovered in a bathing suit that probably cost ten times what it ought to for the two inches of material that it took to make it!

What is considered popular now is to show as much flesh as possible and get away with it. Those women wear that type of clothing for one reason—to be seen! By not dressing conservatively, a woman is encouraging men (sometimes wayward husbands) to look at her in a sexual manner and to become enticed by her, and that is morally wrong. The provocative woman is disrespecting your present or *future* husband—AND herself. Women are not sexual objects, and as women, we need to have more respect for ourselves than giving into the immoral ways of this world.

I know I'm not being very popular right now, but I'm not telling you this to win points with anyone, but to show you that you are NOT scoring any points toward being a Godly woman of virtue.

I know a lot of husbands and boyfriends want to "show off" their woman, but he's doing that woman a disservice by showing off what should be for his eyes only as your present or future husband. You are provoking men to lust after you and worship you instead of God.

Your beauty should not come from outward adornment such as braided hair and the wearing of gold jewelry and fine clothes. Instead, it should be that of your inner self, the unfading beauty of a gentle and quiet spirit, which is of great worth in God's sight. For this is the way the holy women of the past who put their hope in God used to make themselves beautiful. They were submissive to their own husbands, like Sarah, obeyed Abraham and called him her master.

1 Peter 3: 3-6

I want women to dress modestly, with decency and propriety, not with braided hair or gold or pearls, or expensive clothes, but with good deeds, appropriate for women who profess to worship God.

1 Timothy 2:9

The last sentence says it all: you can't worship God and yourself too. By dressing impurely, you are advertising you worship yourself.

32

It's all in your head

Who wears the pants in your family? Unless your answer was, your husband, then I'm afraid you need to rethink this. God did not mean for women to boss their husbands around, yet society tells women they need to have equal rights in everything, whether it be biblical or not.

Wives, submit to your husbands as to the Lord. For the husband is the head of the wife as Christ is the head of the church, his body, of which he is the Savior. Now as the church submits to Christ, so also wives should submit to their husbands in everything.

Ephesians 5: 22-24

Notice it doesn't say to submit to your husband only for the things you feel like submitting to. And it doesn't say to submit only in what society and women's rights agree with. It says to submit to your husband in EVERYTHING.

This does NOT mean you have to do anything immoral or illegal if your husband tells you to, which I pray you won't, and he would never ask. And it also does NOT mean being a doormat. But if you willingly, with a cheerful heart, submit to your husband, it would never feel like you were a doormat.

One day, I was sitting out on the dock at a lake of some friends we were visiting. My husband had gone into the house to get us a couple of bottled waters because it was a hot day, and so he was slightly behind me in making it to the dock. I was already sitting and comfortable by the time he reached me with the water. I heard him come up behind me, but I had my eyes closed, and was getting a little sun on my face. Before he stepped a foot onto the dock, he gave a firm warning: "Honey, don't move!"

Every instinct in me told me to jump up and run screaming from the dock because there was obviously some danger near me I was unaware of. But instead, I trusted my husband and submitted to his demand. There was an upturned row boat only a few inches from where my feet were outstretched on the dock, and my husband had seen a water moccasin slither up out of the water and onto the dock under that boat. I didn't move an inch, though I had NO idea the snake was there until AFTER he stomped across the dock to get it to go back in the water. He'd seen danger that I couldn't see, and if I hadn't been submissive to him, it could have cost me my life. When we aren't submissive to our husbands, it could end up costing us our eternal lives since we're commanded by God to do so.

33

The last word

Don't be the type of person who always has to have the last word. If you are, practice saying it your head instead of out loud. You don't always have to make your point known or understood. Sometimes it's better to keep quiet and let the matter drop, rather than keeping it going just so you can have your point heard.

I've known people that don't listen, but merely wait until you finish so they can say what they have to say, meanwhile, they are missing the point completely. If the entire time your spouse is speaking to you, pouring out his feelings to you, you're spending that time only concerning yourself with your come-back once he's finished, you will never get anywhere when you "communicate".

Your husband's feelings, opinions, and desires are just as important to him as yours are to you, so why would you want to shut him down; especially if he's talking to you? Too many men shut down and won't open up to their wives because they don't feel like their wives really care what they have to say.

{Unfortunately, some of these men will find a woman who will listen to them and give them that emotional intimacy somewhere else. Trust me when I tell you, there are plenty of women who would stand in line to be a good "listener" for your husband, because they feel he's just so *neglected*! (eyes rolling!)}

Do you only want your own agenda? If you constantly have to have the last word, chances are, you do. Maybe it's time to stop talking and start listening. Even if you don't agree with what he says, it's still how he feels and how he sees things. Just because you might not see it that way does not make him wrong. No more than the desires of your own heart are wrong if that's the way you feel—unless your way happens to be self-centered or not in-line with what God expects for married couples. Think about it. If you have to have the last word, chances are, it's because you want your own way too.

Have you noticed how many times I wrote the word "you" in this chapter? Change those "you's" to the word "me" or "I", and see if some of it doesn't apply to you now.

If I've struck a nerve, then it's not too late to turn this around. Take the time to really listen to your spouse, and like I said, have the last word in your head only, where only YOU know it's there, if that's what it takes in order to keep from shutting down the communication between you and your spouse. If the way you handle things and keep taking the last word, don't be surprised if it's the last word spoken in your house for a while.

Silence is only golden if it's not between and angry man and his wife.

Even a fool, when he keeps silent, is considered wise; when he closes his lips, he is considered prudent.

Proverbs 17: 28

34

Let's go shopping

Are you a shopaholic? If you have things in your home that you don't need (we all do), you could have saved that money by not buying that item you thought you couldn't live without, and used it to take your husband on vacation.

You might say to yourself, 'It only cost twenty dollars', but how many other items have you purchased this year that you didn't need?

Humor me and go through your bank account and add up how much you've spent this year on items you didn't need—but wanted. They may sit on a shelf and look pretty, or they may be in your closet with the tags still on them, or perhaps it was too many dinners out that you could have cooked at home instead. A lot of women spend a LOT of unnecessary money on hair salon and nail salon appointments that they really don't need. (remember, it's the inward appearance that is more important than the outer), and if you're more worried about how you look physically than how you look spiritually or how selfish you may seem for spending that money, if you don't have it to spare, then you should take a good look at what you're really spending.

It isn't just money that you're wasting, but opportunity.

If you saved up all the money you spend on salons and unnecessary purchases, you might be surprised how fast it adds up. It could add up to a small trip with your spouse, and quality time with him should be worth far more than those "things" you purchased.

Invest that money into your marriage. Your rate of return is much higher than the satisfaction of looking at something on a shelf you will ultimately have to dust! Don't let your husband be the thing in your life you're blowing the dust from, because that's exactly what you'll be doing if you neglect your husband by spending every little extra bit of money.

No servant can serve two masters, for either he will hate the one and love the other, or he will be devoted to the one and despise the other. You cannot serve both God and money.

Luke 16: 13

35

I did it my way

If you are one of those people who always has to have their own way, you need to reroute your thinking. That is a selfish way to be, and it is not fair to your spouse. If he's always giving into you so he won't have to listen to you wearing him down with nagging until he relents and gives in, that will get old really fast, and he will begin to resent you.

Once this happens, it's hard to reverse it. Instead of making all the plans, or all the rules, ask *him* what movie *he* wants to watch for a change, and if it's something you're not interested in, make yourself watch it with him anyway. If he wants to go golfing and you don't like that, ask him to teach you, or start out playing putt-putt golf until you get to know your short game, then work your way up to driving the ball down the fairway.

In other words, compromising with your spouse on your activities will introduce you both to new things, and will keep you close.

My husband and I do everything together. People ask us why we don't ever get sick of each other, and it all has to do with balance. Where I'm weak, he's strong, and vice-versa. We don't compete with each other, and we cheer each other on always.

We have found things over the years that we both like to do and we concentrate on those things. If he'd gone his way doing what he wanted and I'd have gone my way doing what I wanted, we probably wouldn't ever see each other, and we would have had no idea we liked some of the things we ended up liking. We were lucky from the beginning that we had almost everything in common. People have joked that we are the same person in both male and female form, but that is exactly how God intended all married couples to be. The Bible tells us that when we marry, the two become one flesh—this does not apply only to the bedroom!

We are to be of one mind with our spouses, and of one flesh, knowing that each other belongs to the other. Not in a possessive way, but in a spiritual way so that we will learn to live in peace and perfect harmony with one another.

Before you start calling me a tree-hugger, know that what I'm saying is biblical. You only achieve this level of oneness with your spouse by giving up of yourself. And being one with him is the only way to keep a marriage intact.

Do nothing from rivalry or conceit, but in humility count others more significant than yourselves. Let each of you look not only to his own interests, but also to the interests of others.

Philippians 2: 3, 4

36

Mistake #1

Most of us have a past. A previous boyfriend, and sometimes a previous spouse. ALWAYS remember that person is your ex for a reason!

Unless you have children with that person, there is never a reason to have further communication with your ex. Let it be in the past, and move on with your present spouse. It is never a good idea to be friendly with a person you have a past history with, especially if your spouse is not privy to the conversations, whether in person, text, emails, or phone calls. All that does is invite secrecy and put you in danger of the *appearance* of wrong-doing.

Abstain from all appearance of evil.

1 Thessalonians 5: 22

If you do have children with this person from your past, you should keep civil conversation for the sake of the children, but never continue a relationship with that person during a new marriage. That person should not be your buddy that you go hang out with or have complaint sessions on the phone about your present spouse. Save those conversations for the context of your prayers.

On the same subject, if you had male friends before you married your present husband, it's time to let them go; unless they have wives you can hang out with while your husband now takes over the friendship with the man. I do not advise having friendships with members of the opposite sex when you're married. This could lead to temptation, or could cause misunderstandings that could end your marriage.

You should cling only to your husband, and he should get all of your attention. Leave your past in the past. It became your past for a reason, and maybe you should reflect on that, and not put your present marriage at risk of the chips that might fall from having extramarital friendships.

There is nothing concealed that will not be disclosed, or hidden that will not be made known. What you have said in the dark will be heard in the daylight, and what you whispered in the ear in the inner rooms will be proclaimed from the rooftops.

Luke 12: 2, 3

37

Your nose is growing

Do not lie to your spouse. Period!

Do I have to say it again? Do not lie for any reason, no matter how big or small; even if you think it is to spare his feelings. Sometimes it's better to say something that might hurt for a minute, than to tell a lie that could hurt much more if found out later.

FYI: keeping something from someone is the SAME as lying! If you spent too much at the store and dipped into the savings for it, tell him. If you put a dent in the car, tell him. Whatever it is, it needs to be said.

I tried lying when I was a kid to get out of some trouble, and before I knew it, I was having to come up with one wild story after another just to keep the lies going. Before

I knew it, I'd forgotten the original lie and started to mess it up. Now that I'm an adult, I make it a rule not to lie because God considers a lying tongue an abomination, and I understand why—all lying does is create more problems.

Lies have a way of coming back to haunt us, and no matter what it is, stress to your spouse that you are being brave enough to tell the truth, and pray for the best. Anyone can tell a lie to get out of a jam, but it takes a good, morally sound person to tell the truth, no matter what the consequences.

If you get caught in a lie, it's tough to get out of it.

God truly considers lying an abomination; something he HATES.

Lying lips are an abomination to the Lord, but those who deal truthfully are His delight.

Proverbs 12: 22

Do not lie to one another, seeing that you have put off the old self with its practices.

Colossians 3: 9

38

Money talks

I can NOT stress this enough—save money. Don't spend all you have as soon as you get it. Don't put yourselves in a place where you live paycheck-to-paycheck. Nothing puts more strain on a marriage than not having enough money to pay the bills—especially if one person in the marriage is spending it on frivolous things. Bills ALWAYS get paid first. No exceptions. After that, you should save some for a rainy day. A certain percent should go for tithing, even if you don't attend a regular church.

Tithing can go to many sources, whether it be to a friend who is down on his luck, or a man on the street who is homeless and has nothing to eat. {I can hear many of you squawking at this statement, saying they use that money for drugs or booze}. Not all of them. And as long as you're giving to these people with pure intention, what they do with it after that is between them and God! If you feel compelled to give to one homeless person over another, it's usually because it is a prompting from God, but don't let the enemy trick you into believing all beggars on the street are scammers.

So when you give to the needy, do not announce it with trumpets, as the hypocrites do in the synagogues and on the streets, to be honored by men. I tell you the truth, they have received their reward in full. But when you give to the needy, do not let your left hand know what your right hand is doing, so that your giving may be in secret. Then your Father, who sees what is done in secret will reward you.

Matthew 6: 2-4

39

Mirror-mirror

When you look at your spouse now compared to the day you married him, what do you see? Has his hair begun to gray? Does he have a few wrinkles around his eyes when he smiles? Does he have a spare tire?

What about yourself? Can you still fit into your wedding dress? Have you gotten a little gray or wrinkled? Do you have a permanent scowl on your face?

Whatever shape the two of you are in now should NOT matter. If you no longer find your spouse attractive, shame on you! No matter if it's been six months or six years or more since you married him, if he's changed, chances are you have too in some way.

Maybe it's your attitude that's changed. Perhaps it's something that doesn't show, like your patience with him that has gone down-hill. Whatever it is, if you're not just as smitten with his appearance today as the day you married him, you should pray about this.

My mother used to tell me that beauty is only skin-deep, and she could point out a lot of people who were in need of "skinning"!

Though it's just a saying, there is some truth to it. If our "insides" were laid bare for all to see, we might not be so pretty anymore.

NO, I'm not talking about your guts! I'm talking about your personality and your demeanor. If you're a mean person, or unpleasant to be around, it just makes you ugly. If you're insides are pretty, the rest of you will be pretty no matter what you look like physically.

I used to work with this woman who was really pretty. Her hair was always perfectly in place, and she wore the nicest outfits, but she cussed like a sailor, and thought her middle finger was for showing off to others how unhappy she was with them! She was a beautiful woman until she opened her mouth or started flying her middle fingers like flags!

No one wants to be around someone who is unpleasant, no matter how pleasing they might be to the eyes.

You are altogether beautiful, my love; there is no flaw in you.

Song of Solomon 4: 7

Charm is deceitful, and beauty is vain, but a woman who fears the LORD is to be praised.

Proverbs 31:30

40

I'm not impressed

Do you remember how impressed you were with your spouse when you first met and began dating? This is something that you must remember as the two of you age together. You might have to remind yourself that he's the same man that you married. If nothing else, you should love him more deeply and more unconditionally as time goes by.

If the situation requires it, find new ways to be impressed with your spouse. In the same manner, never stop trying to impress *him.* keep your interest in each renewed every day so that you are not tempted to look elsewhere for something you feel is more interesting.

Love him unconditionally, despite the aging process. Next time you think he might be getting too old for you, take a look in the mirror and you'll see he's just right!

Let your fountain be blessed, and rejoice in the wife of your youth, a lovely deer, a graceful doe. Let her breasts fill you at all times with delight; be intoxicated always in her love.

Proverbs 5: 18, 19

41

To forgive is divine

Don't throw past or present mistakes in your spouse's face. Forgive and FORGET as best you can.

Don't hold onto bitterness and un-forgiveness, because it will hurt you both. You can't expect your spouse to forgive you unless you're willing to forgive him.

Let's not forget the parable of the unmerciful servant…

Then Peter came to Jesus and asked, "Lord, how many time shall I forgive my brother when he sins against me? Up to seven times?"

Jesus answered, "I tell you, not up to seven times, but up to seventy times seven."

"Therefore, the kingdom of heaven is like a king who wanted to settle accounts with his servants. As he began the settlement, a man who owed him ten

thousand talents was brought to him. Since he was not able to pay, the master ordered that he and his wife and his children and all that he had be sold to repay the debt.

"The servant fell on his knees before him. 'Be patient with me,' he begged, 'and I will pay back everything.' The servant's master took pity on him, cancelled the debt and let him go.

"But when that servant went out, he found one of his fellow servants who owed him a hundred denarii. He grabbed him and began to choke him. 'Pay back what you owe me!' he demanded.

"His fellow servant fell to his knees and begged him. 'Be patient with me, and I will pay you back.'

"But he refused. Instead, he went off and had the man thrown into prison until he could pay the debt. When the other servants saw what had happened, they were greatly distressed and went and told their master everything that had happened.

"Then the master called the servant in. 'You wicked servant,' he said. 'I cancelled all that debt of yours because you begged me to. Shouldn't you have had mercy on your fellow servant just as I had on you?' In anger, his master turned him over to the jailers to be tortured until he should pay back all he owed.

"This is how my heavenly Father will treat each of you unless you forgive your brother from your heart."

Matthew 18: 21-35

I don't know about you, but the torture of not being forgiven by God seems even more harsh than any pain we might experience here on earth from sins our spouse or anyone else may commit against us. Refusing to forgive all man's sins against us is not worth losing our eternal life. Likewise, not forgiving your spouse should not be worth losing your marriage over.

42

Monster-in-law

I have only ONE thing to say about mothers-in-law. Learn to love them! Especially if your husband is close with his mother, you need to do everything you can to gain her acceptance. If you refer to your mother-in-law as the *monster-in-law,* stop it—and stop it immediately!

Welcome her as a new member of your family.

This does NOT mean you have to tolerate her meddling in your relationship, or belittling you. Most people would say that it's your husband's responsibility to defend you. To a point, yes, but it is not his fight. If it is a problem between you and your mother-in-law, then it is something you will have to settle with her yourself, and your husband's duty is to back you up, but ONLY if you're right. If you are in the wrong, you need to fix it.

Always be respectful to your mother-in-law (remember that she is your elder, and you should respect your elders).

This is yet another instance where forgiveness is sometimes the ONLY way to settle something. If this requires you to constantly forgive her, then you may end up considering her an "enemy", especially if she's been downright mean to you *without cause*.

I've heard about and experienced both sides of that coin. I have a great mother-in-law now, and I KNOW that she would do anything for me. This is not to say she hasn't overstepped her boundaries a time or two, but it wasn't a fence we couldn't mend. All it takes is a little forgiveness and a LOT of communication.

In the meantime, if it's unfortunate that your mother-in-law is your enemy, treat her accordingly—but do it according to God's word, and do not lash out at her in anger.

Bless those who persecute you; bless and do not curse.

Romans 12: 14

On the contrary; "If your enemy is hungry, feed him; if he is thirsty, give him something to drink. In doing this, you will heap burning coals on his head."

Do not be overcome by evil, but overcome evil with good.

Romans 12: 20, 21

When you are in the company of your mother-in-law, you must be pleasant, for the sake of keeping peace with your husband. Your mother-in-law does not have to be your enemy, but if she treats you like you aren't good enough for her son, you may have to prove to her that you are. In the meantime, for the sake of peace in your home, you can endure a few hours at dinner with her a few times a month, or at family get-togethers.

If she is at your house more often than that, and pushing you around in your own home, or telling you and her son what to do constantly like you have no minds of your own, you will have to set boundaries with her. She needs to know that you are capable of taking just as good of care of her son as she would, and if all she sees from you is a wall of rebellion, she isn't going to trust you.

If, on the other hand, you've shown her that you truly love her son and take good care of him and she fails to recognize this, talk to her BEFORE a civil war breaks out. If you're disrespectful to her, don't expect your husband to back you up. Usually, handling trouble with a mother-in-law is the responsibility of your husband as the head of your house, unless he delegates that chore to you.

Do yourself a favor first…*pray before* you say a word!

After all is said and done, remember, she's YOUR mom now too!

Honor your father and your mother, that your days may be long in the land that the LORD your God is giving you.

Exodus 20: 12

There is an old saying that holds very true, and it goes like this:

A daughter is a daughter all your life, but a son is a son till he gets a wife!

"Therefore a man shall leave his father and mother and hold fast to his wife, and the two shall become one flesh."

Ephesians 5: 31

43

Step-monsters

A word about step-children. They can either be the loves of your life, or they can be thorns in your side. As the adult, that is entirely up to you; I pray you choose to love them as if they were your own. It's unfortunate, but all-too-often step-children are not accepted, and in today's families, it happens more often than it should. If you refer to your step-children as *step-monsters*, you better take a step back and ask God to put love and acceptance in your heart for them—for your sake, the sake of your marriage, but more importantly, for the sake of innocent children who have no choice but to be in that situation. They didn't ask to be put in the place of being step-children, but YOU did because you chose to marry their father; so honor your commitment to him by honoring it to them too!

Occasionally, you will run into problems dealing with jealousy from a bitter ex who does not want you around her children. This makes it even more important for them to have your acceptance.

My brother's ex turned his two daughters against his new wife, despite a very strong relationship they started to have. They got along wonderfully until his ex-wife began to let jealousy turn her kids against their step-mom. It's a sad thing when this happens, especially when that vindictive parent doesn't seem to care that their own children became the real victims—not just the step-parent. As adults, we can overcome such heartache, but little ones are so vulnerable and impressionable, and it hurts them more than it does us.

Never use children or step-children as a weapon to get back at the other parent. There are NO exceptions to this. The children ALWAYS suffer for the bad choices of the adults in these cases.

On the other hand, if you have trouble getting close to your step-children, remember they are a part of your husband. Separate yourself from any animosity there may be between you and the real mother (your husband's ex), and let your relationship with those kids be just between you and them, and forget who their mother is (if you can), and love them because they are a part of your husband.

Innocent children don't ask to be put in that situation, and the easier we can make that transition for them, the better adults we are. They need a strong family foundation, and it's up to you as the adult to provide this for them.

On a side note, if you do not get along with the children's real mother for whatever reason, do not EVER talk bad about their mom to them, or anywhere they can overhear. Such talk should have NO place on the lips of a Christian woman, and you have no right to cause those kids any more hurt than they've already experienced from the divorce between their parents. Be encouraging to them in this vulnerable and scary time for them, and be part of the solution—not part of the problem.

If your spouse's kids give you problems, remember who the adult is! Love them through this time of testing and rebelling, especially if their mother is behind their bad behavior. They are not going to disobey their mother, and you shouldn't expect them to, even if she's teaching them wrong. Pray for them, and always treat them with the same love you do your spouse. After all, they get their good traits from him!

I am fortunate that my husband cares for my son and daughter as if they were his own.

Always show your stepchildren that you love them unconditionally, and make them feel welcome in your home. Be a good, Godly example of a mother—especially if their biological mother is not. This does NOT mean you should upstage their mother, or try to undermine her by teaching them to like you more than her. Like her or not, she will always be their real mother, and you should never try to get in the way of that. They love her, and you have no right to take that away from them.

Enjoy your step-children, no matter what their age, and encourage the relationship your husband has with his children by making room for them in your lives. If your spouse has children, they come as a packaged deal.

Train up a child in the way he should go; even when he is old he will not depart from it.

Proverbs 22: 6

And so train the young women to love their husbands and children.

Titus 2: 4

44

Compliments will get you everywhere

A word to the wise; do not use flattery as a form of manipulation.

If you build up your spouse only to get what you want, you may be barking up the wrong tree. I'm talking about the one you will have to answer to when you stand before God to be held accountable for the careless words you have spoken.

When you compliment your spouse, do it out of love, and be sincere. Tell him how much you appreciate him being by your side in this wonderful journey called life. Good men are few and far between these days, and if you are lucky enough to find one that is committed to being married, you've got yourself quite the catch.

Remember that part of your job as his mate is to make him feel truly wanted by you, and part of that is speaking words that are never harsh, or sound as if they come from a forked-tongue.

For there is no truth in their mouth; their inmost self is destruction; their throat is an open grave; they flatter with their tongue.

Psalm 5: 9

45

Every man's fantasy

Be your husband's EVERY fantasy. Men want a woman who respects them and listens to them; they want a woman who will not treat them like they are inadequate buffoons!

They may act like it, but put yourself in your spouse's place for a minute. How do you suppose he sees you?

Do you nag him all the time? Or are you supportive?

Do you make him feel like he's the luckiest man on earth to have found you, or do you make him regret saying those vows?

Let's be honest here…

Unless you are being every bit the woman you promised you'd be in those vows, you're falling short, and had better step up your game.

Do you love him enough to change the bad habits you've developed? Or do you have the attitude that he better buck-up and catch up with the times?

My prayer for you is that you have the desire to be your husband's EVERY fantasy; in, and out, of the bedroom. If you always put HIS needs above your own, yours will be met too.

Remember the great talks you used to have? He still needs that. Not to spend countless hours talking about all the problems you've developed since your marriage began, but to really talk to him. Talk to him like you used to when you were first discovering each other, and look at him the way you used to. Waggle your eyebrows at him, or grab his caboose as he's walking by and say *woo-woo, all aboard!*

If you continue to show GENUINE interest in your husband physically AND emotionally, you might just discover the next cure for that *seven-year itch,* or the dreaded, *midlife crisis.*

Don't let lack of interest and co-existing to be the death of your relationship.

There is a way that seems right to a man, but its end is the way to death.

Proverbs 16: 25

46

Sticks and stones

Whoever said names don't hurt must not have ever gotten called a name before—or perhaps they were the ones always slinging the poo-words at others.

If you resort to calling names in the heat of an argument, you may say something you regret later on. Once something is said, you can't take it back. It can't be unheard. No amount of apologies can clear it from the other person's mind. You can't strike it from the record. You can't even pretend you didn't say it, and he probably won't be able to pretend he didn't hear it.

Given all that…why would you ever speak a harsh word to your spouse that you could not retract?

Words linger thick in the air, and it takes some words longer to dissipate than others. Some never go away no matter how much you might try to sweep them under the rug. In this instance, it's better not to ever let them escape your lips in the first place.

If words do run loose, you have to pray and ask forgiveness, and even be willing to sacrifice a little to make up for it. Once something is said, you'll be hard-pressed to erase them from your mind, whether you were on the spewing or receiving end of them. *Beg* his forgiveness IMMEDIATELY if you call him a bad name!

My thoughts on this are simple; if you love your spouse, truly love him, you won't call him names because you'll think about it first and know that calling names should be left in the school-yard, and are not called for as grownups in our marriage.

But now you must put them all away: anger, wrath, malice, slander, and obscene talk from your mouth.

Colossians 3: 8

47

Pray without ceasing

By keeping in continuous prayer, we keep our mind so filled with thoughts of the good works of the Lord in our lives; there should be no room for all the things that can hurt our relationship with our spouse.

When we find ourselves out of line with God's purpose for our lives, we may be falsely deceived into thinking everything is just fine and we are doing the right thing, until suddenly we get the wind knocked out of us by some problem that seems to come out of nowhere.

Remember the devil leaves those alone whom he's already gained access, but the more trouble you have flying at you, you better believe you must be on your way to greatness in the Lord—especially if the enemy is working that hard to keep you from it.

When we pray without ceasing, we prevent the devil from getting a foothold in our lives, and can usually ward off any trouble before it becomes something serious or permanent.

Rejoice in hope, be patient in tribulation, be constant in prayer.

Romans 12: 12

Rejoice always, pray without ceasing, give thanks in all circumstances; for this is the will of God in Christ Jesus for you.

1 Thessalonians 5: 16-18

48

I trust you

Trust is a choice! You either choose to trust your mate, or you don't. If your husband has never given you any reason not to trust him—then just do it. Every person is innocent until proven guilty. Even if there is some guilt, if he's willing to try to earn your trust back, do not hold past mistakes over his head.

Forgive the transgression and move on. Unless he repeats the same mistake, never bring it up again. And if he does repeat the offense, only bring up the present incident. Never compile the list of past transgressions, slinging at him that he has done this same thing twenty times now.

Remember what the Bible tells us about how God forgives us. Once it is forgiven, your slate is wiped clean and you are as white as snow, as if the sin never occurred. We have to treat our spouses the same way.

Remember that the measure we use to judge others will be used to judge us. So unless you want God to keep a tally, or your spouse to keep a tally on you, don't do it to him!

Trust is an issue that many of us have problems with. My husband and I both had trust issues from choosing bad spouses previously. But in our own marriage, we were willing to put those trust issues away and start a clean slate with each other, and so far, that has worked for us.

We trust each other because we chose to trust one another.

Trust is a choice! If you don't trust your mate, you are basically calling his love for you and your relationship a lie. So now, not only are you not trusting him, but you're calling him a liar too. Do not add insult to injury in this way. You made the choice to marry him, so you must have trusted him enough.

Most trust issues come from insecurities. I'm here to tell you, insecurities do NOT come from God. The enemy wants to destroy marriages that are strong in the Lord because, together, you are a united force. You are two who have become one in Christ, and for that reason alone, you need to be on your guard—not from your husband, but from the devil playing tricks on your mind and leading you to believe you can't trust the man you sleep next to every night.

If you can sleep soundly next to him, you trust him!

The hardest part of that equation is to convince yourself that the man you chose can be trusted with your heart too. Let love be your guide. If he's broken your trust in the past, give him the room to prove himself trustworthy without you breathing down his neck and holding a magnifying glass up to him examining everything he does. When you try to control like that, you run the risk of pushing him further into whatever it was that broke your trust in the first place.

Therefore, if anyone is in Christ, he is a new creation. The old has passed away; behold, the new has come.

2 Corinthians 5: 17

49

Your wish is my command

Always be ready and willing to do anything for your spouse, as long as it is not something that will physically or morally hurt you or your marriage.

This is something that absolutely baffles me about my husband. I could ask him to climb an icy mountain with me in his bare feet and he would do it—without grumbling!

Wait a minute! What?

No! I would never ask him to do such a thing, but if I asked, he'd do it.

I was so used to getting the opposition from my ex to do anything, I began to realize it was easier to just do it myself than to tolerate his rebellion and resistance.

But now I have this man who is so generous and selfless, that he would do anything for me, and it has made me eager to do the same for him.

I'll admit, I was leery of this when I first met him. But as I got to know the kind of person my husband is; it made me fall in love with him even more. I've made sure that I've honored him by NEVER taking advantage of his good nature.

His ex did that to him, and would demand more when he'd give all he had—going without the things HE needed in order that she could have what she *wanted.* She has tried doing the same since he and I have been married, but we have managed to put her at a distance, and we have both never felt freer.

Be the kind of spouse that will do anything your mate asks of you, but remember, if you grumble about it after agreeing to do for him willingly, it does NOT count! By grumbling, you undo all the good you've tried to accomplish.

Show hospitality to one another without grumbling.

1 Peter 4: 9

Do all things without grumbling or questioning.

Philippians 2: 14

50

Did you pay the electric bill?

Turn off the TV, the computer, and shut off your phones!

Humor me and do this for five minutes! How did it feel? Did it shock you? Were you having electronic withdrawals?

I pray not!

Try eating by candlelight one night a week—even with the kids! Too often, we get so caught up with the conveniences of this day and age that we lose sight of what is really important—quality time with our spouse and family.

If your TV is on EVERY night during dinner, turn it off for a change, and connect with one another. Afterward, play a board-game or play cards, or take a walk.

Devote at least one evening together every week with no electronics allowed. No texting at the table, TV off, and don't answer the phone or the door.

Have an old-fashioned family night. Who knows, you might just start a new trend in your home that will bring you all closer together as a family.

Your wife will be like a fruitful vine within your house; your children will be like olive shoots around your table.

Psalm 128: 3

51

I'm exhausted

You may say to yourself or your spouse; *I'm too tired to clean the house or do the laundry, or (fill in the blank).*

You may have complete justification for not having the energy to do something. It may be that you work a full-time job too, or the children are demanding and still require a lot of work, or it may be that you are having trouble sleeping.

Whatever the reason, always present it to your spouse in a loving and non-threatening manner. He may be exhausted from working overtime to help pay the bills, or he may not be feeling very well, and went to work anyway, and now it's worn him down. You don't know how he's feeling unless you talk it out.

Whatever needs to be done, if your excuse is that you can't do whatever it takes to help keep your house running smoothly, maybe you need to look at your time-management, or it may be as simple as you need to start taking vitamins!

My husband and I have a pact between us. If he's too tired, I will pick up the slack, and if I'm too tired, he does. If we are both too tired, we let certain things go for a time. The house is not going to spontaneously combust if we don't do the dishes as soon as dinner is over, and it won't happen if the lawn gets an extra day of rain before it gets cut.

If you're disciplined and organized, you can make time for work, family, and the chores if you work together.

Put a chart on the refrigerator, and stick to it. Let each day have one chore on it, but remember, if you let something go one day, you have to work extra hard the next day to make up for it.

Pray about your situation if the two of you are burning the candle at both ends. Perhaps it's time to ask for a little help, either from a family member, or the kid down the street that has been begging to mow your lawn for ten dollars, if your budget allows for such a thing. Let him do it once in a while, and you and your husband can take a day off.

If you can't do that right now because of certain restrictions, monetarily, or otherwise, know that God will bless us with the strength to keep going, despite how we may feel about it physically.

I can do all things through him who strengthens me.

Philippians 4: 13

Jesus said, "With man this is impossible, but with God all things are possible."

Matthew 19: 26

She looks well to the ways of her household and does not eat the bread of idleness.

Proverbs 31: 27

52

Road blocks

Sometimes we can be our own worst enemies. If a roadblock occurs in your marriage, create a fork in the road, and move on!

Don't let drama or financial issues, or problems with family (fill in the blank), to put stumbling blocks in your marriage. Whatever is the cause; cut it out—even if it's a family member. If the problem is with a child, decide *together* what to do about the child, and be a united force.

If financial difficulties are causing you stress, and the bills are piling up faster than the money is coming in, sit down together and create a solution. Make a budget, or cut out certain luxuries (no, not like electricity, LOL) that are not necessary until the storm blows over and you get back on your feet.

The two of you not working together to solve whatever problems arise will put a roadblock in your relationship. If your spouse doesn't want to work with you, come up with a solution suggestion on your own, and present it to him *in love.* Never try to force your opinions on him or to demand your own way in something. If a roadblock occurs, it affects both of you, and you should make every effort to solve it together.

And we know that for those who love God all things work together for good, for those who are called according to his purpose.

Romans 8: 28

53

This is your sign

If your spouse is not talking to you because of something you did wrong, this is your signal to do whatever it takes to change it.

Inner changes do not involve trying to change your spouse to adapt or tolerate what you might be dishing out. If your marriage is in trouble, and you helped put it in jeopardy, this is your sign that change needs to happen, and those changes begin with YOU.

Don't concern yourself with what he's doing to change, and don't try to change him. You married him the way he was, leave him be, and let God take care of him!

A compromise might be in order here. Compromise is always best in the situation where neither spouse agrees with the other, and each insists on having their own way. If neither is willing to give in, compromise is the only sane and fair solution for each of you to get your own way—partially.

Trust in the LORD with all your heart, and do not lean on your own understanding. In all your ways acknowledge him, and he will make straight your paths.

Proverbs 3: 5, 6

54

Drop dead diva

Drop the diva act, and put it to death before it becomes the death of your marriage. There is no room in a marriage for one spouse or the other to act like a diva. You are not entitled, the way most of the world thinks they are. One spouse is not entitled above the other. A marriage is an equal partnership.

You must earn respect and give respect. Respect is something you earn, and respect is something you give, it is not something that is just handed to you. And it is not a manipulation tool.

If the relationship is not balanced, one spouse will begin to resent the other, and that is never a good situation. Don't fall on the floor and hold your breath like a five-year-old in order to get your way. You had that right when you were five, and now it's time to grow up. If you don't, it could be too costly.

And to aspire to live quietly, and to mind your own affairs, and to work with your hands, as we instructed you, so that you may walk properly before outsiders and be dependent on no one.

1 Thessalonians 4: 11-12

On a side-note; if your husband forgets your birthday or anniversary, it's because YOU didn't remind him! Yes, I just blamed it on *you!* I see too many women setting up traps for their husbands, and it almost seems as if they *want* their husbands to forget so they can start a fight and play the victim. Please do yourself a favor, and don't be that wife! Don't *lord it over* his head that he forgot, or that he didn't get you what you wanted.

Be content in all circumstances!

Remember that it's your anniversary too, and if you go out and get him a gift, waiting for him to forget so you can hold it over his head (for what? To somehow try to prove you care more about the marriage than he does? That's hogwash!), then fight with him about it, that is NO way to spend your anniversary together.

Not to give your husband an excuse, but men just don't always remember these things the way women do. Remind him your birthday is coming up, and make plans together. And don't throw a fit if he gets you an appliance for your birthday, or Christmas, or anniversary.

Men think more practically than we do. His presence on your birthday should be the best gift you ever got.

The best gift I've EVER gotten was when my husband and I were first dating, and I'd cook for him. Opening cans of black beans for one of his new favorite dishes, I kept cutting my fingers on the edges, despite every attempt to be careful. He went as far as opening them for me, but he took things a step further. One day, on his way over to my place, he stopped at Walmart and bought me an electric can opener that cuts the whole top off the can so there is no sharp edge. The gesture brought tears to my eyes, and to this day, it is the BEST gift I've ever gotten—because he got something I *needed.*

Don't give your husband a list of what to get you for your birthday or other holidays, it takes all the fun out of it, and you might just miss out on such a precious gift as I got!

Trust me when I tell you it still makes me giggle every time I use that can opener, knowing it was the most romantic gift a girl could ever get—much better than flowers that wilt and die away. This gift is a constant reminder of his love for me, and his desire to protect me!

55

Don't ever forget

Most people will say they forgive someone, but they will never forget. I'm telling you to forget and never bring it up again. Don't throw it in his face later, and don't dwell on it.

Move on!

This doesn't mean you can't learn from it. But don't use that as a crutch to hang onto the offense. The Bible tells us that when God forgives us, our slate is wiped clean and we are made new again.

You must apply this same principle in your marriage.

Love keeps no record of wrongs!

Love is patient, love is kind. It does not envy, it does not boast, it is not proud. It does not dishonor others, it is not self-seeking, it is not easily angered, it keeps no record of wrongs. Love does not delight in evil but rejoices with the truth. It always protects, always trusts, always hopes, always perseveres. Love never fails.

1 Corinthians 13: 4-8

56

Don't bet on it

Do NOT use divorce as a threat unless you intend to follow through!

I pray you won't.

If you are constantly threatening your husband that you will divorce him if he doesn't do this or won't stop doing this or that, then you should STOP it and never say it again.

Do I have to tell you about the little boy who cried *wolf*?

Don't even say it in jest. Unless it is an option for you, I wouldn't even entertain the idea. In the same way you should never use sex to get what you want from your husband, you should never threaten to end your marriage.

Next time you're tempted to use the threat, ask yourself if the reason you're threatening is *really* worth losing your husband over. What would you do if your husband had a good comeback for that one? What if he said, '*you know what, I think you're right, I think we should get a divorce!'*.

Think about that for just a moment. If the idea of him divorcing you makes you cry, you better stop threatening it immediately.

Don't ever threaten to divorce him in anger either.

If you are constantly using divorce as a threat to get your own way, you might find out the hard way that your husband will have had enough of hearing it, and might just serve you with divorce papers when it wasn't what you really wanted.

Are you willing to continue to take that chance?

If not, then wipe the word divorce from your vocabulary immediately.

"I hate divorce," says the Lord God of Israel.

Malachi 2: 16

57

Pick your battles

Not everything needs to be discussed, and most certainly, there are things not even worth the effort it would take to fight over!

Sometimes, we need to let go and let God work in our spouses and our marriages, while we pray for guidance.

If you're going to spend your entire marriage picking over the dumbest things that won't matter in ten minutes, you will not only drive your husband crazy, you'll drive yourself crazy trying to get him to stop doing whatever it is that is irritating you.

I could provide you with a long list of things my husband does that irritate me, from leaving lights on in every room, to loading the dishwasher differently than I do so you have to wash more than one load—but I won't. None of that stuff matters enough to waste energy on it. Besides, are any of those things deal-breakers? Absolutely not!

You learn to adapt to those things and accept them because they are all part of what makes your husband into the man you love—faults and all. I've learned to keep my mouth shut and turn off the light after he leaves the room because it takes LESS EFFORT to turn the light off than it does to say something to him, and if I constantly say something then I'm being a nag. I've learned to leave the room when he's loading the dishwasher and just not look. Rather than upset him so he no longer wants to do the dishes, by giving in to my urge to rearrange the dishes after he'd already loaded them *his* way, I LEAVE THE ROOM!

I can't stress this enough: don't be a nag!

If you want his help, let him do things his way; just because he's not doing it the same way that you would do it, does not make him wrong, and it's not hurting anything. Remind yourself that he's willing to take out the trash or do the dishes. And BE THANKFUL!

Always tell him thank you if he does something around the house; even something as trivial as taking out the trash. Be thankful you don't have to do it yourself.

I understand there are MANY men who won't lift a finger at home. If you happen to have one of those men, do NOT nag him to help you, and do NOT resent him.

There are ways to get your husband to help you without nagging.

First and foremost; any issue you present to your husband, do it in love. If you ask him nicely to help you with something, and he refuses because he'd rather watch the football game (or whatever he'd rather do), ask if he'll help at half-time, or every time an ad is on, etc. Or—next time, ask him well in advance of when that game comes on. Do NOT throw a fit and yell at him, or go on strike from making dinner. Simply drop it and do it yourself.

When you serve your mate with a gentle and quiet spirit, he will begin to see what you are doing, and perhaps guilt will settle in, or his sense of duty will kick in, and he'll make up *his own mind* to help you.

If he won't help, don't give up. Ask him every day. If every day he refuses you, do the task yourself. But do it quietly. Don't make a face at him. Don't cry. And don't storm off grumbling that you'll do it yourself because you have to do everything by yourself.

Let it go and let God handle it; you do this by doing the task yourself and praying for God to intervene while you're working.

Do not try to manipulate your spouse into helping you. If he doesn't want to help, no amount of wearing him down will get him to help. It will likely anger him and cause a fight, and that is the last thing you want because that will set the stage for failure to get his help in the future.

You'll lose his help if you allow a civil war to break out over it.

The same goes for anything you want him to stop doing. You can't rub his nose in it and smack him on the booty with a newspaper. If he bites his fingernails, provide him with some hand sanitizer so it doesn't put germs in his mouth. If he leaves the cap off the toothpaste and gets that sticky mess all over, clean it up without a word or making a face, and next time he looks for the toothpaste, it will not be where he left it.

I'm not telling you to give your husband license to be a helpless slob. There will be a time when you might need to present your grievances with him about these things, but give it some time to see if it doesn't fix itself, and if not, say it in love and with prayer, and not when you're angrily cleaning up toothpaste from your bathroom counter.

Then the LORD God said, "It is not good that the man should be alone; I will make him a helper fit for him."

Genesis 2: 18

58

Drama queen

The only place drama belongs is on the stage! Our lives are so full of drama; there is no reason to create more. The world is full of it.

Women who feel the need to create drama in their marriage should love their husbands with a quietness and gentleness instead. If a woman feels the need to embellish situations to be dramatic in order to gain attention or be heard, that can end up backfiring and become a BIG turnoff to your husband. Instead, try being quiet and not making a bad situation worse by adding drama to it. You might just end up being heard more by being quiet!

You don't need to be the center of attention all the time, and you don't need to *act up* in order to get attention from your spouse. By adding drama, all you do is get negative attention from him, and that is probably not what you want.

Instead, have a quiet and gentle spirit, and be soft-spoken. Trust me when I tell you, men find this far more attractive. They laugh at the drama queen putting on her show of disapproval with the world, but it is the respectable woman who gets taken home to meet the parents.

Get rid of your crown, and adorn your head with humility, and your husband will step back and take notice. When you stop having snappy comebacks and act classy instead of (insert rhyming word here…don't make me say it), then you'll probably find you're a lot happier and freer. Being a drama queen comes with a LOT of baggage! That drama crown has got to be heavy!

Once you lose the crown, you can hold your head up and be the sort of Godly woman you promised in those vows you said to him when you married him.

But if you bite and devour one another, watch out that you are not consumed by one another

Galatians 5: 15

59

Your cheating heart

The scripture tells us that if a man looks at a woman lustfully, he's already committed the adulterous act in his heart.

This principal does NOT apply only to men!

If you are drooling over your neighbor's husband because he likes to go outside and wash his car in short shorts, showing off rippled muscles, and you are married to a short, skinny, fat, balding, (fill in the blank) man, then you have to remember you chose your husband; perhaps not for his physical appearance, but for his heart.

Remember that you love your husband.

Ask yourself if your husband knew what you were thinking about this man, would it hurt him?

If the answer was yes, and let's be honest, unless your husband does NOT love you whatsoever, he cares!

"You shall not covet your neighbor's house; you shall not covet your neighbor's wife or his male servant or his female servant or his ox or his donkey or anything that belongs to your neighbor."

Exodus 20: 17

When we covet, we are sinning. No two ways about it.

On the contrary, if you're watching a TV show only because all the men on the show are *hot,* then you're committing sin in your heart.

If you are watching, talking to, entertaining, or *harmlessly* drooling over, or flirting with ANY man who is NOT your husband, you are sinning.

No exceptions!

If you are guilty of this, confess it in prayer and ask God to give you eyes for your husband only. Ask for a renewed heart and the self-control to reject temptation. If you are guilty of this, confess it in prayer and ask God to give you eyes for your husband only. Ask for a renewed heart, and the self-control to reject temptation.

"You have heard that it was said, 'You shall not commit adultery.' But I say to you that everyone who looks at a woman with lustful intent has already committed adultery with her in his heart.

Matthew 5: 27, 28

The wisest of women builds her house, but folly with her own hands tears it down.

Proverbs 14: 1

60

Dinner time

Don't use the time you have together to sit down to a meal, to do anything other than to eat that meal and enjoy each other's company.

Turn the TV off. Don't talk about work or money problems or the kids; unless they are there, which in that case, you should be setting a good example for them. Make it fun, and use that time to really connect.

When I was growing up, my father would love to tell jokes at the table, much to my mother's verbal disapproval. Every night was joke night at dinner, and those are some of the fondest memories I have of growing up—listening to my dad's corny jokes during our meal. And even though we were on the low end of middle class, we were dressed and washed for dinner every night!

Dress up for dinner and make it special. There are many ways to make your dinnertime special and memorable.

Dinner time should always be family time.

Beloved, let us love one another, for love is from God, and whoever loves has been born of God and knows God.

1 John 4: 7

61

I'm not a mind reader

This is where communication comes in most handy. Don't expect your husband to be a mind reader. If you don't tell him what you need, and tell him and in love, he won't know. In the same respect, if you don't tell him, you have no reason for getting angry that he doesn't already know what's wrong with you, or what your needs are.

All too often women are quick-tempered when it comes to their husbands not knowing what they need. But you can hardly hold that against him if you don't tell him. And if you *have* told him a thousand times, perhaps you told him at the wrong time, or in the wrong tone of voice. My husband told me that when his ex would tell him things, she was always so angry and patronizing he couldn't listen past the screaming, or the belittling and pure hostility in her tone. As a result, he just didn't comprehend what she would say to him, and then she'd be angry because he couldn't repeat back to her what she'd said. This was all *after* she expected him to know what she was thinking even though she hadn't said anything to him. She would get angrier still because he didn't just automatically know.

Are you kidding me?! It makes me angry just thinking about her yelling at him because he's a very gentle and patient person—and an awesome listener!

There is never a reason for either spouse to yell at the other. You're not your spouse's parent—he's the love of your life, and you should treat him as your equal, not as if he's below you. That's all yelling accomplishes; it establishes a superiority over the other person, and there is no place for it in marriage.

My point here is that you must communicate with your spouse, and I can't stress this enough; communicate in a tone he won't tune out. I liken that to blowing a dog whistle and expecting your husband to come running to your side. Not gonna happen!

You have no right to expect him to automatically know, just because you've been together X number of years, and he should just know you that way. That sort of mentality does neither of you any good at all.

Use your words, and use them wisely.

Know this, my beloved brothers: let every person be quick to hear, slow to speak, slow to anger;

James 1: 19

Likewise, wives, be subject to your own husbands, so that even if some do not obey the word, they may be won without a word by the conduct of their wives.

1 Peter 3: 1

Sometimes it's better just to be quiet together. You don't have to know what your spouse is thinking all the time, and sometimes, it's better to keep your own thoughts to yourself, especially if you're not happy with each other for some reason.

This does not mean you should throw communication out the window.

62

Great expectations

Learn to let go of your expectations, because if you don't, your spouse will fall short of them every time, and that's not fair to him. There is NO such thing as a perfect marriage, except between us and God. No earthly marriage is perfect, despite the fact that some people make it look so easy.

Remember that YOU chose him, so if he fails to meet your expectations, that's on you, not him. Unless he turned into a Dr. Jekyll and Mr. Hyde after you married him (unfortunately, my ex did just days after I married him, but that's for the next book LOL), then he should measure up.

If you put him on a pedestal before you married him, then it's your job to keep him on that pedestal—in your eyes, anyway. He may get old or fat or gray, but as long as you love him the same, if not more when all that happens, then you have knocked him off that pedestal, causing him to no longer measure up.

It all goes back to loving him unconditionally.

If you set your expectations at a realistic level, you won't be disappointed, and you might even get a nice surprise if he should ever exceed those expectations.

In the same respect, you should strive to exceed your husband's expectations of *you.* Be a much better wife than he could have ever hoped for. We should always strive for perfection in ourselves, and not hold others to that, to keep from having feelings of regret. I hear so many couples complaining that they've fallen *out* of love with one another, and they are contemplating divorce. I'm sorry, but you can't just trade him in for a new puppy just because you don't like the old dog. If you've gone through a cycle with your husband, work on changing how you see him.

If you've become annoyed by every little thing he does, maybe you should take a step back and ask yourself how you're seeing him. If you've lost tolerance and patience for him, you need to change YOU not him. I guarantee you he's the same person; it's *you* who's changed.

Anyone who does not love does not know God, because God is love.

1 John 4: 8

Love bears all things, believes all things, hopes all things, endures all things.

1 Corinthians 13: 7

63

It's comfortable

Don't get so comfortable in your marriage that you forget to maintain it. If the two of you spend more time in separate parts of the house than you do together, or if it seems like you've become two people merely existing in the same residence, it might be time to pay some attention to your marriage.

If you've settled into a routine of soccer practices and ballet recitals, or PTA meetings, or perhaps two full-time jobs between you, and there is no room left to be a couple—stop what you're doing and take inventory of when you have time to squeeze even a few minutes of down-time with your spouse. If you don't maintain your relationship, it will suffer, and you could begin to drift apart.

The time to remedy that is BEFORE it becomes an issue.

Spending quality time with your spouse when you have a hectic schedule is not always easy, but sometimes you have to take a step back and ask yourselves if you're *too* busy, and why. Is there an area in your lives where you can manage your time a little better?

It is so important to have a *date night* with your spouse, but you each have to be willing to set aside time for it. If you can't afford to go out, make your date night in, but make sure it's after the kids go to bed, or you can have a relative keep the kids. Sometimes it's easier to have intimate moments with your spouse if the kids are out of the house, so find inventive ways to keep them busy with relatives or friends, such as offering to pay for a pizza night or movie night. That can often be cheaper than paying for a babysitter so you can go out and spend even more money. Save time and money by staying in, and having your house to yourselves.

Don't be too tired or caught up in your busy schedules to make time for your marriage. Get dressed up—even if you're having dinner at home. Put on a little music and dance. If the two of you haven't danced since your wedding, it's time!

If you don't take the time to nurture your marriage, the sparks will die out, and then you'll just be two people who have the same address in common.

Submit to one another out of reverence for Christ.

Ephesians 5: 21

64

A bigger piece of the pie

I think one of the best things about my husband (and he'll tell you the same about me), is that we would each give each other the largest slice of pie and take the smaller piece for ourselves, or even give up the last piece to the other (we usually end up splitting a small piece LOL).

We were both married previously to such selfish people, we often joke that the two of them would be perfect for each other! Too often, one spouse does all the taking, while the other does all the giving. We should always strive to do more for our spouse, and take his feelings into consideration above our own, and in turn, our own needs will be met.

If you are out there getting your nails done, while your husband is going to work in socks that have holes in them and he has to be on his feet all day, you should feel ashamed. Whatever the situation is that you are giving your spouse the short end of, stop it. Trust me when I warn you, he will get tired of going without while you live in luxury and ease.

Take a quick mental inventory.

Look around your house; do you have all the trinkets you want all over the house, forcing him to live in a feminine environment, or does he have his own space (a man-cave), or at the very least, a garage that looks manly? Or does every space in your house—including your bedroom, look as if NO man lives in your house?

Is your husband still wearing the same clothes he had when the two of you met, while you have two closets full of clothes, most of which still have the tags on them?

Do his socks and underwear have holes in them, while you get the most expensive bras and underwear from a designer store? (you know the one I'm talking about!). When the two of you go out shopping, do you get things more often than he does, and is the money spent on him unbalanced?

Shame on you—especially if he's the sole breadwinner. He doesn't work for *you,* he works for the two of you as a couple. Next time you go to spend that money selfishly, ask yourself a very REAL question: how many hours, or days, weeks, months, years (pick one!) will my husband have to work to pay for this?

If even his most basic needs are not being met in order for you to have everything, that is a problem.

Be a giver, not a taker.

Do nothing from rivalry or conceit, but in humility count others more significant than yourselves. Let each of you look not only to his own interests, but also to the interests of others

Philippians 2: 3, 4

But if anyone has the world's goods and sees his brother in need, yet closes his heart against him, how does God's love abide in him?

1 John 3: 17

65

Your serve

When my husband and I each got married previously, we were told some *ugly* words by our new spouses—almost immediately after the wedding.

His ex said to him; *I hope you don't think you married your mother.* Translation: I'm never going to do a single thing for you—and she didn't!

My ex said to me; *I PAID for you!* Translation: you're going to do everything I say, and get nothing in return. It was true!

We must ALWAYS be in the mindset to be submissive and subservient to our spouse. We are to love them and do for them as we would do for ourselves. There is no room in your marriage for selfishness. We are to be submissive to one another, and in doing so, our needs are met too.

If your spouse does something nice for you, thank him and pay it forward. Repaying good with evil is against God's word.

But if anyone does not provide for his relatives, and especially for members of his household, he has denied the faith and is worse than an unbeliever.

1 Timothy 5: 8

66

The bedroom scene

Every marriage requires a certain amount of intimacy, but I'm not just talking about sex. You need to have a deep, emotional connection with your spouse for things to work right in the bedroom.

The only way to achieve that is to love one another unconditionally. A lot of couples suffer their own anxieties in the bedroom, and unless you connect emotionally and physically, it might not be the best experience for one or both of you.

If things are not in balance in the bedroom, they will cause problems in the rest of your marriage. True intimacy starts with your emotions. If you have a good relationship with each other, which comes from having a close, personal relationship with God, then everything in the bedroom should fall into perfect order.

Don't be afraid to explore a little, and don't be selfish in the bedroom. Most of all—don't fake your enthusiasm with your husband (you know what I'm talking about ladies!). If you can't genuinely respond to your husband's love-making to be sure it's pleasurable for both of you, then you need to talk things out, and perhaps try a different approach or position that is more comfortable and more pleasing. If you fake your way through sex, you aren't doing anything but putting distance between you and your husband. In the end, all that does is cheat you out of what is rightfully yours as a wife.

Wives, submit to your own husbands, as to the Lord.

Ephesians 5: 22

Being naked in front of your spouse does not merely consist of being without clothes. I'm referring to exposing your true self to your spouse. Don't be stingy with who you are to your husband. Open up to him—even if you've been hurt in the past.

You need to trust him and give him that honor as though he's the first man you've ever trusted.

67

Green-eyed monster

Jealousy is an unacceptable and ugly trait in ANY relationship.

In today's social-media driven society, it's easy to get an inside look at what others do and have. When we want everything that everyone else has, we lose the ability to be content, and God requires us not to covet what others have, and to be content in our circumstances. When we want what others have, we give the devil a foothold in our lives. Learning to be content with whatever our circumstances, takes work.

There is nothing wrong with striving for more, whether it be a bigger house if your family is outgrowing the one you're in, or a more reliable car. It's when we become jealous and even hateful toward others for having things we don't have, that it becomes a problem in our lives. Pray that you will be content with what God has entrusted you with, and your measure will be increased.

If jealousy stems from insecurities, these can also wreak havoc in your marriage. Whether justified or not, deep-rooted insecurities about our abilities to make our spouses as happy as someone who is smarter, younger, healthier, prettier (fill in the blank), play a big part in destroying a lot of marriages.

Ask yourself what is the root of your insecurities.

Does your spouse have a wandering eye, or perhaps a flirtatious personality? If so, talk this over with him in love. On the other hand, if there has been infidelity in your marriage, this can cause you to feel fear that it may happen again, and could cause you to drive away your spouse with accusations. Unless there is proof-positive that this type of problem exists in your marriage, it's best to pray about it, and ask God to put forgiveness in your heart for whatever you *think* he may have done, or what he may have done in the past. If you've decided to forgive the infidelity, forgive it, and don't bring it up again. The constant reminder of his sin may drive him to give up, feeling it's no use to turn away from that sin when he's constantly being accused for his past sin.

Ask God for a healing of your insecurities and to remove the fear you feel associated with the jealousy.

If problems of infidelity plagued a previous relationship, don't blame your new spouse for his sins, especially where there isn't any guilt. Don't accuse him of doing the same thing the previous spouse or boyfriend did if there is no justification. Being fearful that he *might* do the same thing in your relationship is a FAR cry from the actual act, and he does not deserve to be accused for another man's sins. If you have this sort of problem in your marriage, it may be wise to consider talking with your Pastor, or other counselor who might be able to help you work out these feelings.

This world is full of depravity, and unless you and your husband walk around with blinders on, you're going to come in contact with it.

If you are jealous of someone else's marriage, you may need to look inward and evaluate your own relationship with your own husband. Have you given up on him or your marriage? Other's marriages may seem like they are closer or healthier because those spouses may be concentrating on their own relationship and working hard at maintaining that love between them.

Strive for the same thing without being jealous of other women because their husbands appear more attentive than your own, or whatever the reason is behind your jealousy. It's usually not true that the grass is greener on the other side; things may not always be what they seem.

Stop concerning yourself with what others are doing, and keep your eyes on God and your husband. Sometimes, being oblivious to the world around us can help keep our concentrations on what God wants us to focus on in our lives.

For where jealousy and selfish ambition exist, there will be disorder and every vile practice.

James 3: 16

But if you have bitter jealousy and selfish ambition in your hearts, do not boast and be false to the truth. This is not the wisdom that comes down from above, but is earthly, unspiritual, demonic.

James 3: 14, 15

Be kind to one another, tenderhearted, forgiving one another, as God in Christ forgave you.

Ephesians 4: 32

And if he sins against you seven times in the day, and turns to you seven times, saying, 'I repent,' you must forgive him."

Luke 17: 4

68

A gentle answer turns away wrath

I can't stress enough that you should never have any cause to yell at your spouse. Even if he does something that makes you so angry you could spit; don't give in to the urge to yell.

First of all, it accomplishes nothing. Secondly, no one likes being yelled at, so don't do it. If he begins to yell, keep your voice even-toned. Show him you aren't willing to have a knock-down-drag-out brawl with him. Instead, be quiet and loving; with forgiveness at the ready *before* you begin to discuss the matter.

Whenever dealing with our spouse on sensitive matters, always ask yourself how *you* would feel if you were on the other end of your talk. Don't talk over your spouse, and try to out-yell him. If he's the only one yelling and your answers are quiet, chances are, he's going to calm down. Raised voices only make matters worse, and a raised voice implies superiority over the other. It is best to avoid this at all cost, but it is dependent on you having self-control over your own tongue.

A fool gives full vent to his spirit, but a wise man quietly holds it back.

Proverbs 29: 11

A soft answer turns away wrath, but a harsh word stirs up anger.

Proverbs 15: 1

For this very reason, make every effort to supplement your faith with virtue, and virtue with knowledge, and knowledge with self-control, and self-control with steadfastness, and steadfastness with godliness.

2 Peter 1: 5, 6

Set a guard, O LORD, over my mouth; keep watch over the door of my lips!

Psalm 141: 3

69

Grow up!

There is no room in a marriage for one spouse to act like a helpless child, expecting the other one to carry the entire weight of all the responsibility.

When I was a child, I talked like a child, I thought like a child, I reasoned like a child. When I became a man, I put the ways of childhood behind me.

1 Corinthians 13: 11

If you happen to be in a marriage where your spouse is an *absent* partner, you must be careful not to let resentment set into your heart.

This might be another area where you might have to *pick your battles* with your spouse, and let a LOT go.

Stop and ask yourself these questions:

1. Does he have a job that he goes to regularly?
2. Does he contribute to the household bills?
3. Is he loving toward you, the kids, the in-laws, etc.?
4. Is he a good spiritual example?
5. Does he usually clean up after himself?
6. Does he mow the lawn or take out the trash (anything considered by most to be "man's work")?

If you answered *yes* to these questions, then ask yourself if it's really worth starting a civil war just because when he's home from work he wants to relax and leaves most of the responsibility on your plate. That's okay! You've got a good foundation to work with. The rest may come later. Pick your battles.

If, on the other hand, you answered no to one of them, most, or even all, you may have a problem that is beyond the advice of this book, in which case, my suggestion would be to start with your Pastor or another counselor you trust.

In a third scenario, if YOU are being the irresponsible one who won't contribute anything to the relationship, I want to speak directly to you as the wife. There are certain things that a good wife does for her husband and family, and those include, but are not limited to:

1. Keeping the home tidy and clean
2. Keeping everyone in clean clothes
3. Cooking healthy meals
4. Being a partner to her husband

5. Being a primary caregiver to the children

There are other ways you can contribute, such as clipping coupons to save money on expenses, etc. I believe the woman's number one role in her home is to keep her husband happy. Do you know that old saying that says, *if momma ain't happy, nobody's happy?* I believe the opposite is true. If your husband is happy, you and your children's needs will be met, and everyone is happy.

70

Deliver us from temptation

Temptation in a marriage can be a dangerous thing. There are many forms of temptation, but I'm going to address the issue of fidelity here.

More and more women are getting addicted to pornography, or indulging in extramarital affairs. Another danger is flirting or getting emotionally involved with another man. A lot of women will tell you it's just a harmless flirtation, but there is nothing harmless about flirting with or getting emotionally attached to a man who is not your husband.

My husband and I each had spouses who cheated on us during our marriage. It was not fun to be in that situation from our end. If you're thinking of cheating, think of how your husband would feel if he found out. How would YOU feel if you found out your husband cheated on you?

I'm telling you straight-up that the hurt and betrayal an affair causes the other spouse is catastrophic. My ex actually told me that he felt guilty the *first* time, and after that, he felt numb and empty. Though he admitted regret, he never apologized.

There are many risks involved in having an affair:

- Divorce is likely inevitable
- Sexually transmitted disease
- Pregnancy
- Domestic violence is likely
- Losing custody of your children
- Losing a job
- Guilt and shame
- Weakening of your faith

I could probably go on, but I think you get the picture.

My personal thoughts are that if you aren't happy with your spouse, and you want to cheat, be decent enough to let him go before hurting him in such a way, so that he can move on and find someone who will be true to him.

If you've been tempted, and don't want to go through with the act, then I applaud you. But know this; the enemy will continue to tempt you. Be armed with God's word. If you feel you can't overcome this temptation alone, PLEASE seek help from your Pastor or another counselor.

Finally, pray over your marriage, and avoid any further contact with the person who is tempting you.

RUN THE OTHER DIRECTION FAST!

No temptation has overtaken you that is not common to man. God is faithful, and he will not let you be tempted beyond your ability, but with the temptation he will also provide the way of escape, that you may be able to endure it.

1 Corinthians 10: 13

Flee from sexual immorality. Every other sin a person commits is outside the body, but the sexually immoral person sins against his own body.

1 Corinthians 6: 18

71

Eating crow

Eating crow is a lot harder to swallow than humble pie. Don't wait for your spouse to serve it up to you, humble yourself before it's too late, admit your wrongs, and cut your losses.

If you wait for your spouse to dish it up, it will be far tougher to swallow.

When we refuse to admit wrong or accept responsibility for wrongdoing, it causes our spouse to distrust us. But there are actually benefits to confessing when we are wrong:

- Lifts guilt and burdens
- Restores trust
- Diminished risk of repeating the mistake
- Feelings of relief
- Restores your conscience

- Restores respect
- Makes you accountable

If you've made a mistake, and who hasn't, never be afraid to admit it and ask forgiveness. You should make it a practice to always admit wrongs—especially before your spouse finds out. It will pave the way to a smoother relationship.

"Admit your faults to one another and pray for each other so that you may be healed."

James 5: 16

72

That's going to Leave a mark

Every time you resort to name-calling in your marriage, you put a permanent mark on your relationship that rarely goes away. If you make snide remarks or call hurtful names, those will stick in your spouse's mind, and they are impossible to erase. If he should repeat the offense, no matter how small or large, he will associate fear of being called that same thing, and it may cause him to stumble when he might not have otherwise.

He may even fear ridicule from you if he should make a mistake that you'll call him the name again. He'll hear it in his mind as if you just said it, even though it could have been months since you uttered the (should-be) unspeakable words.

If you're constantly flinging poo-words at him, don't be surprised if they come back at you full force, and before you know it, another civil war has broken out in your home. Try to avoid this at all cost.

"So whatever you wish that others would do to you, do also to them, for this is the Law of the Prophets."

Matthew 7: 12

73

Man's best friend

Be your husband's best friend. Be his biggest cheerleader. And most of all, be in his corner at all times.

If we only stick around when the going is good, and can't see him through late hours of studying to get a promotion at work, or give him encouragement when he feels like he's just not able to give anymore to a thankless job he hates, then we're only hurting ourselves in the end.

Any time you do not stand firm with your husband in his convictions, you are putting distance between you. He needs to know that you support his dreams and his plans for your future.

After all, it's your future too, right?

So why would you do anything that could sabotage that? When you support him, his support for you should naturally come back to you.

If you have dreams, share them with him.

So then, brothers, stand firm and hold to the traditions that you were taught by us, either by our spoken word or by our letter.

2 Thessalonians 2: 15

74

Time's up

You cannot drag your feet when it comes to fixing your relationship if it's in trouble.

If for some reason, you don't feel safe with your husband, such as violent outburst, or possible mental issues, get help from an outside source, whether it be your doctor, or even law enforcement, if necessary.

As much as I hate to admit, there are some problems that are just too big for us to handle alone. If you require outside help for your marriage, even if it's only a marriage counselor; if you love your spouse and want to stay in the marriage, fix it fast.

Love him through problems that come up—especially if you are both willing to stay in the marriage and fix things.

For at one time you were darkness, but now you are light in the Lord. Walk as children of light.

Ephesians 5: 8

75

I love you to the moon and back

Love your spouse unconditionally, and by that, I mean, without finding fault in him whatsoever. No matter how imperfect he is, you are also imperfect, and should remember that. You should also remember how attracted you were to him in the beginning, and find that attraction again. You can't afford not to. He's the same person you met and fell in love with. You married him.

Love comes with no conditions. Period.

Therefore, my beloved, as you have always obeyed, so now, not only as in my presence but much more in my absence, work out your own salvation with fear and trembling, for it is God who works in you, both to will

and act for his good pleasure. Do all things without grumbling or questioning, that you may be blameless and innocent, children of God without blemish in the midst of a crooked and twisted generation, among whom you shine as lights in the world, holding fast to the word of life, so that in the day of Christ I may be proud that I did not run in vain or labor in vain.

Philippians 2: 12-16

Beloved, let us love one another, for love is from God, and whoever loves has been born of God and knows God. Anyone who does not love does not know God, because God is love. In this the love of God was made manifest among us, that God sent his only Son into the world, so that we might live through him. In this is love, not that we have loved God but that he loved us and sent his Son to be the propitiation for our sins. Beloved, if God so loved us, we also ought to love one another.

1 John 4: 7-11

76

Be all that you can be

Giving 100% in your marriage is the ONLY way it will work.

Marriage takes work.

Let me say that again: marriage takes work!

You have to be willing to suffer and rejoice with each other; it can't all be fun and games.

Real life isn't like that!

Love endures all things.

More than that, we rejoice in our sufferings, knowing that suffering produces endurance, and endurance produces character, and character produces hope, and hope does not put us to shame, because God's

love has been poured into our hearts through the Holy Spirit who has been given to us.

Romans 5: 3-5

Love is patient and kind; love does not envy or boast; it is not arrogant or rude. It does not insist on its own way; it is not irritable or resentful; it does not rejoice at wrongdoing, but rejoices with the truth. Love bears all things, believes all things, hopes all things, endures all things. Love never ends. As for prophecies, they will pass away; as for tongues, they will cease; as for knowledge, it will pass away.

1 Corinthians 13: 4-8

77

Proverbs 31 woman

If you truly want to be the best wife for your husband, you will read Proverbs 31 daily and ask God to apply the principles in your own marriage to ensure a long and happy marriage. Here is the scripture for you:

The Wife of Noble Character

10 A wife of noble character who can find?
She is worth far more than rubies.

11 Her husband has full confidence in her
and lacks nothing of value.

12 She brings him good, not harm, all the
days of her life.

13 She selects wool and flax and works with eager hands.

14 She is like the merchant ships, bringing her food from afar.

15 She gets up while it is still night; she provides food for her family and portions for her female servants.

16 She considers a field and buys it; out of her earnings she plants a vineyard.

17 She sets about her work vigorously; her arms are strong for her tasks.

18 She sees that her trading is profitable, and her lamp does not go out at night.

19 In her hand she holds the distaff and grasps the spindle with her fingers.

20 She opens her arms to the poor and extends her hands to the needy.

21 When it snows, she has no fear for her household; for all of them are clothed in scarlet.

22 She makes coverings for her bed; she is clothed in fine linen and purple.

23 Her husband is respected at the city gate, where he takes his seat among the elders of the land.

24 She makes linen garments and sells them, and supplies the merchants with sashes.

25 She is clothed with strength and dignity; she can laugh at the days to come.

26 She speaks with wisdom, and faithful instruction is on her tongue.

27 She watches over the affairs of her household and does not eat the bread of idleness.

28 Her children arise and call her blessed; her husband also, and he praises her.

29 Many women do noble things, but you surpass them all.

30 Charm is deceptive, and beauty is fleeting; but a woman who fears he LORD is to be praised.

31 Honor her for all that her hands have done, and let her works bring her praise at the city gate.

Proverbs 31:10-31

Turn the page to see the sneak peek of Book 2…

till DEATH
Straigh Talk to Husbands: After the "I do"
Katie King

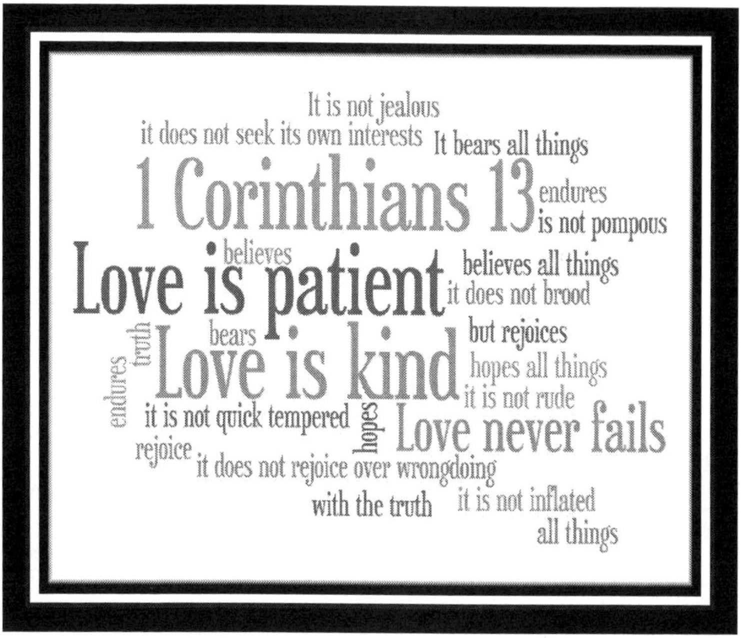
It is not jealous
it does not seek its own interests
It bears all things
1 Corinthians 13
endures
is not pompous
believes
Love is patient
believes all things
it does not brood
truth
bears
but rejoices
endures
Love is kind
hopes all things
it is not rude
it is not quick tempered
hopes
Love never fails
rejoice
it does not rejoice over wrongdoing
with the truth
it is not inflated
all things

Please check out my fiction titles.

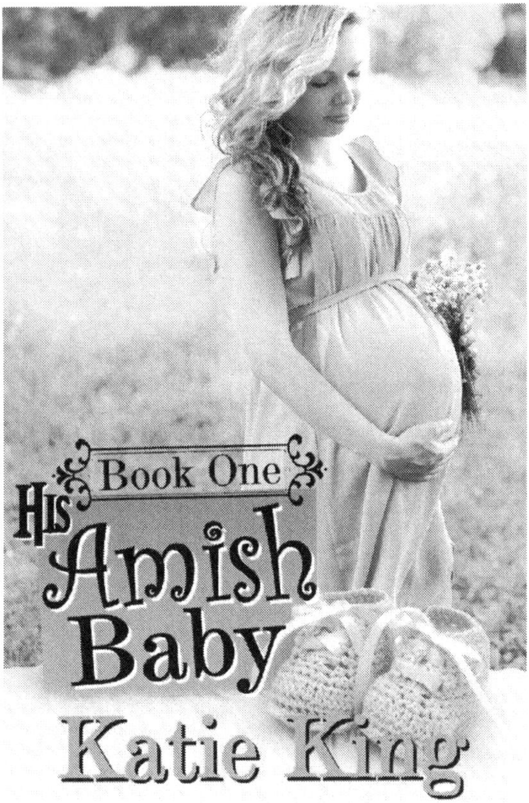

Book Two
His Amish Baby
Katie King

55138295R00124

Made in the USA
Lexington, KY
12 September 2016